The Future is Digital

George Rzevski

The Future is Digital

How Complexity and Artificial Intelligence will Shape Our Lives and Work

 Springer

George Rzevski
Rzevski Research Ltd.
London, UK

Complexity Science and Design
The Open University
Milton Keynes, UK

ISBN 978-3-031-37809-6   ISBN 978-3-031-37810-2   (eBook)
https://doi.org/10.1007/978-3-031-37810-2

Cover Illustration: © Anita Ponne / stock.adobe.com

This Springer imprint is published by the registered company Springer Nature Switzerland AG
The registered company address is: Gewerbestrasse 11, 6330 Cham, Switzerland

Paper in this product is recyclable.

Preface

Motivation

I wrote this book to articulate in nontechnical terms the results of my research into patterns of ever-increasing complexity of the socioeconomic environment in which we live and work.

In simple terms, the pattern is: *social evolution favours complexity; when complexity increases, we invent new tools for resolving issues caused by the latest increase; new tools, in turn, change society.*

Artificial intelligence (AI) is the latest tool for resolving issues created by the most recent surge in complexity. The corollary is: those who delay or ignore AI will be overwhelmed by complexity.

Recognising an enduring pattern in a seemingly chaotic socioeconomic situation is reassuring—it provides a firm foundation on which to base decisions that will affect vital aspects of our life.

Such reassurance was particularly important at the time when I conceptualised the book. A prolonged stable and prosperous period enjoyed by the world ended abruptly. The global financial crisis of 2008, the Covid pandemic of 2020 and the invasion of Ukraine by Russia of 2022 caused the interruption of global supply chains and shortages of energy and food and triggered a sharp increase in inflation.

There was a need for an informed clarification and prediction of the outcome.

Content

The book starts with a broad description of *coevolution of technology and society* that irreversibly leads to the sharp increase in complexity of our socioeconomic environment. The key differences between the *society of hunters and gatherers, agricultural society*, current *industrial society* and the imminent *digital society* are highlighted.

The second chapter covers concepts and principles of the new *science of complexity* which helps us to understand issues caused by socioeconomic complexity—frequent unpredictable disruptive events, butterfly effects and drifts into failure—and provides methods for resolving them.

A beginner's guide to *artificial intelligence* helps readers to glance at fundamentals of this new powerful technology capable of resolving issues created by socioeconomic complexity. The danger of allowing intelligent digital systems to make high-risk decisions is discussed as well as the consequences of possible misuse of AI for fraud and fake. The possibility of AI outgrowing and dominating the human race is considered.

The concepts of *natural and digital ecosystems* are explored and illustrated by examples. Digital transformation of rigidly structured corporations and administrations into adaptive and evolving organisations is illustrated by a number of case studies.

The current hectic *transition of industrial to digital society* is described, and its origins are identified and outcomes predicted, highlighting issues created by the increase in complexity and showing how to resolve them using thinking tools such as complexity mindset and digital tools such as artificial intelligence.

The last two chapters outline my *vision of the future digital economy and digital society*.

Some parts of the book have been written from the UK perspective, but its message is valid globally.

All chapters in the book are more or less self-contained and could be read in any order.

Intended Readership

The intended readership are *decision-makers* in politics, business, administration, banking, policy making, education, healthcare and defence and *their advisors*. The book is meant to help them to contribute to the creation of the brave new digital world.

The content may also help *investors* to recognise which elements of digital technology will play the most important role in the near future.

To gain from reading this book, no previous knowledge of digital technology is required.

The book is accessible to all who are curious to glimpse into the future.

London, UK   George Rzevski

Acknowledgements

The author acknowledges contributions to research and development of emergent AI software by Professor Petr Skobelev from Samara, Russia. We have worked together for more than 30 years, often spending endless hours immersed in debates how to resolve a complex issue. Petr led a high-quality team of more than 80 programmers who coded most of the systems listed in Chap. 4.

Professor Asoka Karunananda from Moratuwa University, Sri Lanka, and his talented development team made important contributions to the AI-based Singhalese-English translator software, which we developed over several years of working together in Colombo and London. Asoka, with the author's help, founded in Colombo more than 20 years ago the Sri Lanka Association for Artificial Intelligence, the first AI association in Asia.

Dr Petros Gelepithis, Dr Mirce Knezevic, Dr Agnes Kaposi, Professor Jeff Johnson, Jan Wouter Vasbinder and Tamara Rzevski Moore read early drafts of the manuscript and made valuable comments.

Contents

About the Author

George Rzevski is Emeritus Professor, Complexity Science and Design Group, The Open University, Milton Keynes, UK, and previous Visiting Professor at Cologne University of Applied Sciences; Wuhan University, China; Samara Aerospace University, Russia; Moratuwa University, Colombo, Sri Lanka; and Brunel University, West London.

Until his retirement in 1999, George was Head of Department of Design and Innovation and Director, Centre for the Design of Intelligent Systems. His Centre was well funded by grants from government and industry, and his Department was rated 5 out of 5 in the two Research Assessment Exercises. At The Open University, George pioneered undergraduate education in intelligent mechatronics, launching a course in which every student experimented at home with their own personal intelligent robot.

His extracurricular activities included assessing candidates for tenure on behalf of a number of American universities, including Stamford, Ohio and Texas; examining over 30 PhD students from universities in the UK and abroad, including Cambridge University, Imperial College, LSE, Royal College of Art, Cardiff University, Singapore University, National University of Ireland and Moratuwa University, Colombo; and delivering regular series of lectures on Economic, Social and Cultural Implications of the Internet to postgraduate students at the London School of Economics. For many years, he was Editor-in-Chief of the journal *Artificial Intelligence in Engineering*, published by Elsevier.

Professor Rzevski has published widely and delivered keynote papers at numerous international conferences. As a tribute to his successful research career on his retirement, The Open University named his research laboratory as "George Rzevski Complexity Laboratory".

Since retiring from The Open University, Professor Rzevski founded and managed a number of small businesses which designed, coded and delivered AI systems on order.

Rzevski Research Ltd, London, www.rzevskiresearch.uk, is his current business through which he conducts research in broad areas of complexity science and artificial intelligence, designs emergent AI systems and offers consulting services in digital transformation. His recent consulting projects include Digital City, for a prosperous Swiss metropolis, and Digital Insurance, for one of the largest Australian insurance companies.

George was born in 1932, in Serbia, into a Russian family of emigrees evading the October Revolution.

He is alumnus of Belgrade University and Imperial College, London.

1

Coevolution of Technology and Society

Introduction

Social order and technology are closely interlinked as illustrated by the diagram below. Society affects the evolution of technology, and technology, in turn, affects the evolution of society, the process known as *coevolution of society and technology* [1] (Fig. 1.1).

Like natural evolution, the *socio-technological coevolution has no goal and no objectives*. Technology changes society in an unpredictable and irreversible manner, and the process is not only difficult to recognise but impossible to influence by the participants. By the time the individual participants realise what the consequences of the massive use of new technology are, it is too late to stop or modify the process.

And, of course, changes are always resisted, and even denied, by those who enjoyed significant benefits under the disappearing order, but the process is unstoppable. The interaction of society and technology is quite logical:

Society invests into creative minds that invent new tools (technology).
New technology creates new jobs and destroys many old ones.
New jobs create new businesses (and, from time to time, new economy).
New businesses change the social order.

G. Rzevski, *The Future is Digital*, https://doi.org/10.1007/978-3-031-37810-2_1

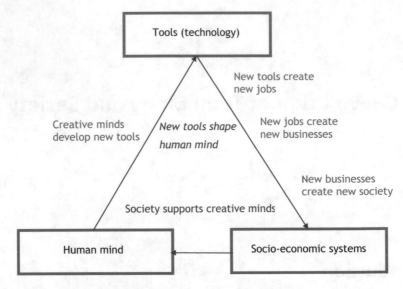

Fig. 1.1 Irreversible coevolution of technology and society

New Tools Drive Social Evolution

Since time immemorial, tools have changed those who invent them and those who use them.

The discovery of fire and the invention of stirrups are good examples of the power of tools (technology) in shaping society.

Approximately 2 million years ago, homo erectus learned how to control fire and, as a result, improved their diet. Proteins helped the human brain to expand significantly in size, and the human race was propelled to the top of the food chain by the newly developed supremacy of human intelligence. Furthermore, gatherings around the fire created cohesive communities [2].

The second example is less dramatic but still very impressive. The invention of stirrups, first used in France around the eighth century, helped mounted warriors keep their balance when fighting on horseback and consequently contributed to the creation of the medieval social class of knights, significantly affecting social evolution [3]. According to Burke, [4], the use of stirrups in the Battle of Hastings in 1066 by attacking Normans significantly contributed to their victory and, consequently, to a fundamental transformation of political and economic environment on the British Islands.

A simple invention—dramatic consequences.

Three Major Socio-technological Transitions

In recorded history there have perhaps been three pulses of change powerful enough to alter Man in basic ways. The introduction of agriculture... The Industrial Revolution... (and) the revolution in information processing technology of the computer....
    Herbert A. Simon

The diagram in Fig. 1.2 shows three of the most important stages in social evolution: agricultural society, industrial society and digital society.

At every transition, the socioeconomic *connectivity* has increased significantly, pushing *complexity* to a higher level [5].

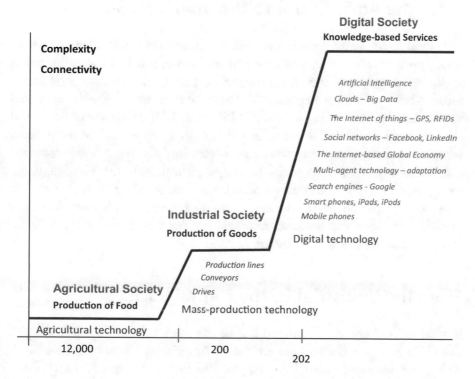

Fig. 1.2 The increase of social connectivity and complexity at every major social paradigm shift

From the Society of Hunters and Gatherers to the Agricultural Society

Agricultural technology, which includes all the knowledge and tools necessary for cultivating large areas of land, was developed approximately 12,000 years ago in Lebanon and Anatolia and quickly spread around the world, enabling hunters and gatherers to abandon a nomadic existence and settle down in permanent dwellings. The transition to agriculture led to a truly radical social change. Loosely organised tribes of hunters and gatherers were replaced by a rigidly structured hierarchical society with a relatively small number of land-owner families at the top and, at the bottom, millions of manual agricultural workers living in poverty [6]. Traders, retailers, bankers, doctors and estate managers formed a small middleclass.

The key economic resource of the agricultural society was *land*, and, consequently, *landowners formed the social and political elite.*

From the Agricultural to the Industrial Society

Industrial technology, which enabled manufacturing and distribution of goods on a massive scale, was invented and developed in England, starting with the invention of the steam engine by James Watt and the first steam locomotive by George Stephenson. The entire *Industrial Revolution* lasted approximately 100 years, between 1750 and 1850. Consequential social changes were dramatic. To work in the industry, people had to move from villages to towns, where they were paid better, initially living in overcrowded conditions without proper social security and healthcare [7]. Gradually, the living conditions for industrial workers improved, certainly in the West.

As *money* replaced land as the key economic resource, landowners lost their prominence—*bankers, investors, industrialists, lawyers, professional politicians and press barons entered the establishment.*

From the Industrial to the Digital Society

Digital technology was developed late in the twentieth century, primarily in the USA. Key contributors are almost all Americans, Vinton Cerf and Bob Kahn, the Internet; Steve Jobs, Apple; Bill Gates, Microsoft; Larry Page, Google; Mark Zuckerberg, Facebook; and Jeff Bezos, Amazon, with a significant input from the UK—Tim Berners-Lee, the World Wide Web. Many digital technology start-ups have proliferated, initially, primarily in the USA and the UK.

Digital technology includes familiar devices, such as computers, smartphones, tablets, pod music players, digital tags, the Internet, the World Wide Web (www), broadband, Wi-Fi, 4G and 5G networks, artificial intelligence (AI) and a variety of other hardware and software systems and applications.

The widespread implementation of the new technology took place in the twenty-first century.

The Internet, smartphones, the Internet-based global market, social websites and the Google search engine were embraced by consumers and businesses with unprecedented speed and enthusiasm.

The Digital Magic

When digital technology was invented, it seemed that its main purpose would be to advance computational practice. It turned out that the power of digital technology is much more universal. In fact, the reasons why digital technology emerged as the key transformational force for our economy and society have nothing to do with computing. The magical secrets of the Digital Revolution are:

1. Digital communication (smartphones and the Internet) has increased the socioeconomic *connectivity* and, consequently, *complexity* of the economy and society causing unprecedented issues.
2. Digital intelligence (AI) turned to be the only tool that can *resolve the thorny issues created by complexity*—a paradox—digital technology boosts and tames complexity.
3. Digital coding enables the capture, storage, transmission and reproduction of texts, images, sounds and movements with incredible speed and precision, enabling digital systems to *autonomously perform intellectual work* such as *knowledge processing* and to facilitate the *cost-effective trading in knowledge*.

Rapid Acceptance of Digital Technology

As illustrated in Fig. 1.3, since the beginning of this century, the widespread use of digital technology and consequent increase in complexity of our

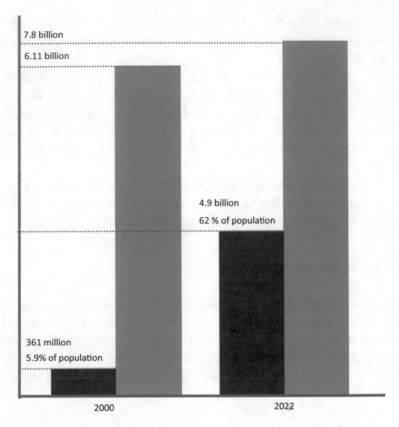

7.8 billion

6.11 billion

4.9 billion

62 % of population

361 million

5.9% of population

2000   2022

Fig. 1.3 The recent sharp increase in the number of Internet users

socioeconomic environment have been truly staggering. Within 22 years, we experienced the penetration of digital technology into our everyday life and work.

In the year 2000, only 361 million people used the Internet, but by 2022, the number of users increased to an astonishing 4.9 billion (out of the total world population of 7.8 billion). With its 2 billion websites, the Internet self-organises and evolves displaying adaptability and resilience to disruptions and cyberattacks.

Through the Internet, nearly 4 billion people are connected to *social digital media*, where they are given opportunities to express their views, display details of their life, engage in debates and create relationships, forming a vast complex socio-technological system. The fact that some contributors to the social media often abuse each other and wage cruel wars of words (cancel culture) should not detract us from noting that a large majority of social media users act responsibly, respecting constraints imposed by norms, rules

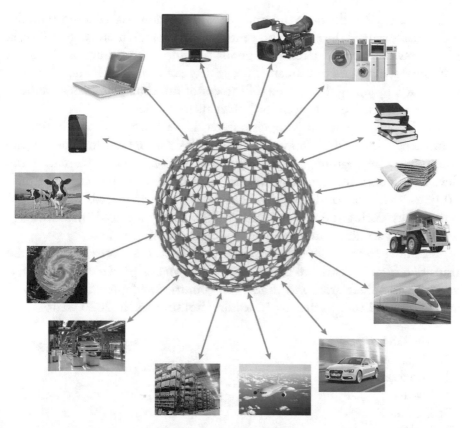

Fig. 1.4   As many as 4.9 billion people, 40 billion physical objects and at least 35 trillion pages of documents are connected to the Internet

and the law. We can view the social media system as a new version of a village—*a global village*—and a nasty gossip was always an integral part of most villages.

The Internet-based *global market* is a genuine complex system connecting an estimated 3 billion of individuals and almost all businesses. Suppliers, customers, lawyers, accountants, traders, brokers, wholesalers, retailers, consultants, bankers and investors are engaged in creating, modifying and cancelling transactions with unprecedented speed, making forecasting of demand and supply unreliable (Fig. 1.4).

There is no doubt that the use of digital technology will accelerate, creating a huge number of new employment opportunities, which, in turn, will change the existing and create new businesses and, eventually, create a new *digital society*.

The process is analogue to the emergence of the industrial economy and the industrial society in the eighteenth century. Then, it took more than 100 years for manufacturing and trading in goods to replace agriculture as the main economic activity and to dismantle the society dominated by landowners and aristocracy, installing the new establishment of full-time politicians, bankers, investors, industrialists, lawyers and media personalities.

The Digital Revolution is moving faster. If we consider the invention by Tim Berners-Lee of the World Wide Web in 1983 as the starting point of the Internet and the beginning of the Digital Revolution, my guess is that, in the developed world, the transition will be, more or less, completed in less than 60 years, that is, around 2040. By that time, the current establishment that got wealthy during the industrial era will be largely replaced by knowledge workers that acquired eminence driving digital transformation.

According to the well-respected Huawei Global Connectivity Index, the transition from industrial to digital society, known as *digital transformation*, is very uneven. There are frontrunners (20 countries), adopters (37 countries) and starters (22 countries). The 10 leading frontrunners in 2020 were:

1. The USA
2. Singapore
3. Switzerland
4. Sweden
5. Denmark
6. Finland
7. The Netherlands
8. The UK
9. Japan
10. Norway

Germany (15th) and France (16th) were somewhat lagging. China (41st) and Russia (50th) were quite behind.

In the digital economy, the key economic resource is *knowledge*, or *intellectual capital*, replacing the money, the main economic resource of the industrial economy. This shift becomes obvious, when we recall that in the industrial economy, those who had money could buy any knowledge they needed, whilst in the knowledge economy, the opposite is true—those who have unique knowledge can choose where and how to obtain capital required to turn their knowledge into a commercial product or service—as Bill Gates, Steve Jobs, Jeff Bezos, Mark Zuckerberg and Elon Musk did.

Peter Drucker named the new digital society the *post-capitalist society* [8].

We are gradually, imperceptibly and irreversibly leaving the capitalist economy in which capital was the key economic resource and entering the digital economy in which knowledge is replacing money as the secret of prosperity.

Three Revolutions and Four Distinct Societies

We know that the differences between the society of hunters and gatherers, agricultural society and industrial society are quite radical.

Hunters and gatherers lived in small tribes, moved from time to time in search of better environment and enjoyed a reasonable equality.

In contrast, the agricultural society was characterised by a small, powerful and rich elite of landowners ruling over millions of underprivileged agricultural workers and a growing, but still small, middleclass of traders, estate managers and professionals such as lawyers, teachers and medical doctors.

Industrial society brought a significant increase in living standards to workers employed in manufacturing and created a new and immensely prosperous elite of bankers, investors and supporting professionals, such as lawyers, business executives and politicians, pushing landowners from the main stage.

In a short space of time, the industrial economy managed to reduce the power of aristocracy that ruled the world for thousands of years.

However, a significant downside of industrial age was that, by chasing profits through the economies of scale, businesses and administrations ignored a basic human need to live and work in smaller units. Large and rigid corporations and huge hierarchical administrations are the legacy of this short episode in social evolution. Large factories were built in countries far away from demand points—globalisation—requiring a huge quantity of goods to be transported up and down the planet, wasting energy, damaging nature and endangering national security during global crises such as pandemic or war.

How different will be the new digital society?

The trends are detectable. We can expect to see:

Digital transformation of traditional corporations and administrations into smart digital ecosystems that are adaptive, resilient and sustainable

Reduced global trading in goods and increased exchange of knowledge based services

Strengthening of nations as the more or less self-contained economic units that compete or cooperate with each other through physical and digital networks

Knowledge replacing capital as the key economic resource

Table 1.1 Main socioeconomic features of four distinct societies

	SOCIETY OF HUNTERS & GATHERERS	AGRICULTURAL SOCIETY	INDUSTRIAL SOCIETY	DIGITAL SOCIETY (projection)
KEY ECONOMIC ACTIVITY	hunting and gathering	agriculture	production and trading in goods	exchanging knowledge-based services trading in knowledge
KEY TECHNOLOGY	simple tools & weapons	agricultural technology	mass-production technology	digital technology, artificial intelligence
KEY RESOURCE	hunting and gathering skills	land	capital	knowledge, intelligence, intellectual capital
KEY SUCCESS FACTOR	tribe management	labour management	economies of scale	adaptability
DISTRIBUTION	none	local roads	railways, motorways, sea routes	digital networks, the internet
SCOPE	tribal	local	international	global
ESTABLISHMENT	tribal elders	landowners	bankers, industrialists, lawyers, politicians	knowledge workers
MANAGEMENT	team-centred	autocratic	centralised, hierarchical, command-and-control, top-down, vertical	decentralised, distributed, participative, cooperative and competitive

Dominance of knowledge workers (defined by Peter Drucker [9] as a new class of workers who rely on their intellectual abilities and expertise to perform their job tasks as scientists, engineers, doctors, lawyers, educators and many others whose work is primarily focused on generating and applying knowledge and information) replacing professional managers and professional politicians as the main decision-makers

Gradual takeover of the social and political establishment by leaders of digital transformation (Table 1.1)

Key Points

1. As society evolves, new issues arise, which the well-established technology cannot resolve. To resolve new issues, we invest into new technology.
2. New technology, by opening up previously unavailable opportunities, changes the employment patterns which, in turn, change society.

3. As Herbert Simon wrote, we experienced "three pulses of change powerful enough to alter Man in basic ways". The three new technologies that were powerful enough to radically change society are:

- Agricultural technology, which enabled *cost-effective cultivation land* and empowered landowners
- Industrial mass production technology, which enabled *highly productive automation of manual work* and empowered bankers, investors, industrialists and professionals who support them
- Digital technology, which is capable of performing *autonomous intellectual work* (such as coding knowledge and making decisions under conditions of uncertainty) and is empowering knowledge workers

4. Coevolution of technology and society is irreversible and unstoppable, and during lengthy radical transitions, it is rather uncomfortable. But invariably, when the transformation is completed, working and living conditions improve. There is much to be gained by completing the transition early. We would be well advised to focus on racing into the digital future.
5. As the agricultural society switched to industrial and then to digital, the key economic resource also changed—land was replaced by money, and money is being now replaced by knowledge.
6. Throughout the social evolution, those who controlled the key resources formed the socio-political establishment. Knowledge workers are next in line.

References

1. Rzevski, G. "Coevolution of Technology, Business and Society", International Journal of Design & Nature and Ecodynamics, Volume 13 No. 3 (2018), pp. 231-237. ISSN: 1755-7437.
2. Wrangham, R. "Catching Fire: How Cooking Made us Human". Basic Books, New York, 2009.
3. White, Lynn, JR. "Medieval Technology and Social Change". Oxford University Press, 1962.
4. Burke, J., "Connections". Macmillan, 1978.
5. Rzevski, G., "Complexity as the Defining Feature of the 21ˢᵗ Century". International Journal of Design & Nature and Ecodynamics. Volume 10, No 3 (2015), pp. 191-198. ISSN: 1755-7437.
6. Mazoyer, M., Roudart, L., "A History of World Agriculture". Taylor & Francis, 2006.

7. Allen, Robert, "The British Industrial Revolution in Global Perspective", Cambridge University Press, 2009.
8. Drucker, Peter, "Post-Capitalist Society". Butterworth-Heinemann, 1994.
9. Drucker, Peter, "Landmarks of Tomorrow"

2

A Gentle Guide to Complexity

The 21ˢᵗ century is the century of complexity.
Stephen Hawking

Introduction

Every important aspect of the twenty-first-century world is *complex*—volatile, everchanging, unstable and with unpredictable outcomes. Here is a representative list: global political constellation, religious and military conflicts, the Internet-based global market, mass migration and pandemic.

Let's make an effort to master the basics of complexity. It will help us to comprehend current global and national problems and to figure out how to solve them.

What Is Complexity?

The word *complex* derives its meaning from the word *plex* (interwoven or interconnected) and should not be confused with similar words such as "complicated" (as a jet engine), "cumbersome" (as bureaucracy), "unwieldy" (as an ageing empire), "chaotic" (as a disorderly administration) or "difficult to understand" (as a verbose document).

"Complex" is a scientific term [1].

A situation or a group or, more formally, a system is complex if it consists of a large number of diverse, partially autonomous participants (called agents), engaged in intense interaction among themselves and with their environment without being centrally controlled.

Complexity is as old as the world. What is new is the *current sharp increase* in social connectivity and, therefore, in complexity, driven by the widespread use of digital technology, primarily the Internet and smartphones.

Let's consider two examples of complex systems, one from the eighteenth and another from the twenty-first century.

A moderately complex system is a cattle market with, say, 100 sellers and buyers negotiating sales of 100s of cows. The interaction of sellers and customers is not centrally controlled, and the outcome of a market day—which cattle will be purchased by whom and which will remain unsold—is uncertain. A typical complexity of the eighteenth century.

A typical complexity of the twenty-first century is exemplified by the Internet-based global market, with billions of participants negotiating deals, with a click of a mouse. The dynamics of such a system is such that the supply and demand equilibrium is impossible to reach. The system, when disrupted, has no time to return to the initial state—the system operates "far from the equilibrium" or even "at the edge of chaos".

Examples of complex systems, which have emerged through evolution, rather than by design or planning, include biological systems (human brain), natural ecosystems (forests, grasslands, rivers, oceans) and social systems (democracy, mass migration, terrorist networks, markets).

In a complex system, *autonomy* (freedom to decide what to do) of participants is restricted by membership rules, the legal system and norms of behaviour.

The overall behaviour of a complex system is *uncertain* (unpredictable) because it emerges from the interaction among participants, and yet, it is not random; it follows *discernible patterns*.

Therefore, the key skill required to succeed under conditions of complexity is *pattern recognition*. And to be able to recognise patterns, we need *intelligence, both natural and artificial*.

Sources of Complexity

Complexity of a system increases with *connectivity* and *autonomy* of participants. The greater the participant's ability to connect with other participants and the greater their freedom to choose how to act, the higher the complexity. The *strength* of connections between participants is also important. Weak connections, which can be easily broken and new ones established, increase complexity [2].

Table 2.1 Complex versus deterministic and random systems

RANDOM	COMPLEX	DETERMINISTIC
uncertainty = 1	1 > uncertainty > 0	uncertainty = 0
full autonomy	participants have partial autonomy	no autonomy
disorganised	selforganising	organised
unpredictable behaviour	emergent behaviour	predictable behaviour
examples: movement of molecules, roulette	examples: game of football, global economy, climate	examples: jet engine, clock

Complexity and Uncertainty

Every activity around us is either deterministic, or complex, or random.

Let's use uncertainty as the demarcation criterion for distinguishing complex systems from deterministic or random [3], as shown in Table 2.1.

Uncertainty is a consequence of complexity, and it increases with complexity. Low-complexity systems have uncertainty close to 0, whilst highly complex systems have uncertainty close to 1—they are *at the edge of chaos* [4] (the word chaos is used here to mean random behaviour).

Complexity Issues

Complexity causes problems only if it is imposed upon us by external factors which are not under our control. The main problem is the increased uncertainty of living conditions, caused by:

1. *Frequent unpredictable disruptive events*
2. *Occasional extreme events*, caused, for example, by the *butterfly effect* or *a drift into failure*

Let's look at the causes one by one.

Frequent Unpredictable Disruptive Events

As referred to earlier, the Internet-based global market in which billions of suppliers, customers, middlemen, investors, bankers, consultants, advisers and speculators negotiate new deals and alter or cancel previously agreed deals, at unprecedented speed, represents a typical present-day high-complexity system.

Organisations operating in this market experience frequent, unpredictable *disruptive events*—nonarrival of expected orders, arrivals of unexpected orders, cancellations or modifications of orders, delays, human errors, failures of resources and electronic fraud and hacking.

The frequency of disruptions is such that these organisations, unless equipped with rapid decision-making AI systems, suffer losses.

Early in the 2000s, I was invited to advise one of the largest car manufacturers in Europe on how to deal with the high volatility of car markets. The client had, at the time, 45 car factories around the world, including some of the biggest mass production plants in Europe, supported by very large and expensive computer-based production planning systems, which had to work all night to plan the daily production. The problem was that as production went underway, every hour or so, the client would receive a stream of messages from dealers cancelling or modifying orders. Since the car production could not be changed as quickly as orders, but had to proceed as planned, a certain percentage of manufactured cars could no longer be delivered to car dealers and had to be parked outside, waiting to be sold at discount. The author rapidly assembled an international group of highly competent software developers and built for the client a prototype real-time scheduler, driven by artificial intelligence, which managed to demonstrate that it is feasible to reschedule affected parts of the production within minutes of the arrival of a modification or cancellation of an order (disruptive event). But the client was unable to switch to the new, real-time scheduling because the physical production infrastructure, built following principles of the industrial economy, could not be adapted to cope with frequent changes of production schedules. And it was much too expensive to develop a new adaptive production system.

There are exceptions, as always, factories producing baby nappies or car batteries do have a continuous and stable demand even in complex markets.

Occasional Unpredictable Extreme Events

In complex systems with nonlinear relations between components, such as the climate, the smallest disturbance, such as movement of a butterfly wing, may cause, at the other end of the planet, an extreme event—a storm—the phenomenon known as *butterfly effect* [5] or *black swan* [6].

Butterfly effect is the most dangerous aspect of a complex system. The amplification of small disturbances is difficult to discover, and there is uncertainty as to when the accumulation will reach the *tipping point* and create an extreme event.

The most dramatic case of the butterfly effect was the recent coronavirus pandemic—a single meal of an infected animal or, possibly, a single mistake in a virus laboratory, which enabled a population of viruses to escape—that triggered a rapid propagation of the virus through the highly connected "global village", causing worldwide infection, millions of deaths and economic disruption on a huge scale.

Due to high connectivity of both participants, the Russian invasion of Ukraine in 2022 has rapidly translated into worldwide economic and political crisis.

A drift into failure is another dangerous aspect of complexity but easier to handle than the butterfly effect [7].

When a complex group (see definition on page 22) operates successfully over a long period of time, a tendency may develop among constituent participants to neglect some of their duties or engage in small-scale illegal activities, which can be individually easily concealed. However, the consequences accumulate over time, and when the tipping point is reached, an extreme event (a failure) is triggered.

The financial crisis of 2008 was caused by a drift into a failure [8]. The accumulation of small toxic loans (loans that could not be repaid), approved to gain bonuses, gradually reached the tipping point and turned into an unstoppable global crisis.

The evidence gathered from experiments with complex digital systems shows that to prevent drifting into failure, it is necessary *to impose a strict control of the behaviour of complex system participants when the operation is going smoothly but to allow them a considerable freedom of action to encourage creative thinking, during the recovery*—the exact opposite to what was done by the UK and US financial authorities during the build-up to the crisis and during the recovery.

The Power of Complexity

When complex systems are under our jurisdiction, or we are in charge of designing them, we can adjust levels of complexity to suit our purposes and harness many useful features of complexity.

Certain properties of complex systems are almost miraculous and can be used to substantially improve performance of any organisation. *Emergence,* self-organisation and *coevolution* belong to this category.

Let's explore this further.

Emergence

Complex systems have remarkable *emergent properties*—properties that are present in the system as a whole and not present in any constituent component. These properties *emerge* from the interaction of components of the system. Perhaps the most obvious example of how useful emergent properties are is the *teamwork*. The ability to solve problem by a team is always superior to the sum of abilities of team members.

Human intelligence is an emergent property of the human brain. No part of the brain is intelligent—intelligence emerges from the interaction of neurons. And so do creativity and self-awareness.

Emergent intelligence, both human and digital, is the silver bullet of the digital age.

Emergence is particularly useful in artificial (man-made) complex systems such as complex adaptive software—you can imagine the excitement when my team discovered emergent intelligence in a *complex software* designed to schedule a rather difficult road transportation business [9]. Complex software is a network of thousands of short algorithms, called *digital agents*, which exchange messages among themselves discussing how to produce the best schedule under everchanging conditions. In that respect, complex software is akin to the human brain. Our complex software was given a task to schedule the loading of cargo onto trucks of various capacities under unusually difficult circumstances. At some point, the agents unexpectedly decided to try a brilliant, original move that at a stroke solved a difficult problem.

Let me emphasise, digital agents were not instructed by the programmers what to do—on the contrary, they surprised the programmers with their decision. A clear proof that complex software can create emergent intelligence.

Self-Organisation

Self-organisation is the capability of a complex system to autonomously (without external intervention) reconfigure its resources to meet a new demand, reduce consequences of a failure, repel an attack, prevent fraud, resolve conflicts or improve its performance [10, 11].

Self-organisation makes complex systems *adaptive, resilient and sustainable*.

Can we ask for more?

Adaptability is the capacity for self-organising in response to a *disruptive event* (cancellation or modification of a demand, arrival of an unexpected demand, failure of a resource, a no-show). The adaptive system autonomously identifies a disruptive event and reschedules affected resources to neutralise, or at least reduce, the consequences of the disruption.

An adaptive scheduler, in response to a request, allocates a minicab to a passenger and continues monitoring traffic conditions; if it detects a sudden traffic congestion affecting the scheduled vehicle, it rapidly reschedules the fleet of affected minicabs to avoid the delay in collecting the passenger.

Conflict resolution is a capacity for self-organising to resolve a conflict caused by two or more demands requesting access to the same set of resources at the same time. A complex system resolves a conflict by trial and error, and it (1) identifies a conflict; (2) assumes that certain adjustment in the demand will resolve the conflict; (3) makes the adjustment; (4) evaluates results and, if necessary, modifies the initial assumption; and (5) repeats steps 3 and 4 until a mutually agreed resolution of the conflict is achieved or resources available for conflict resolution run out.

Two clients asked for their cargos to be delivered to a warehouse at the same time. The complex system that managed deliveries autonomously decided to ask one of the clients if the delivery could be delayed or moved forward. Permission was not given, and the system approached the other client, who agreed. The conflict was simple, but the important point here is that the system made a sequence of autonomous rapid decisions, which resolved the conflict.

Resilience is the capacity for self-organising in response to a *fraudulent or malevolent attack*. The resilient system autonomously identifies an attack and reschedules affected resources to neutralise or, at least, reduce the consequences of the attack (approval of a toxic loan, illegal transfer of money, hacking, cyberattack).

A well-known bank experienced a night attack by hackers, who managed by the morning to withdraw money from thousands of customer accounts (a real case). It is a clear instance of negligence—the bank neglected to build resilience into its systems. An AI-based protective system would monitor transactions by customers 24 h a day, would immediately note that the repeated emptying of accounts is an irregular activity and would rapidly close the bank website.

Spontaneous self-improvement is the capacity for self-organising to improve own performance. A complex system self-improves by trial and error: it (1) detects a weak aspect of system performance; (2) assumes that a certain change in resources will improve system performance; (3) implements the change; (4) evaluates results and, if necessary, amends the starting assumption; and (5) repeats steps 3 and 4 until the desired performance improvement is achieved or resources available for self-improvement run out.

A complex adaptive scheduler, which allocates trucks to transportation orders, after completing the schedule with some time to spare, discovered that some large trucks were not fully loaded; it autonomously found newly available smaller vehicles and rescheduled the transportation order using the more appropriate trucks.

Creative destruction is a capacity for self-organising when the system realises that its performance cannot be improved piecemeal. The system destroys offending part of itself and then rebuilds it using a different building method.

A complex system for the allocation of aircraft to air charter flights found that it could not match an available aircraft to any flight demand. It destroyed the schedule and began the allocation from the beginning, now matching flights to aircraft (rather than aircraft to flights), and the problem was solved.

Coevolution

Complex systems have a propensity to *coevolve* with their environment—they self-organise to accommodate changes in their environment, and the environment self-organises, usually almost imperceptibly, to accommodate the changes in constituent systems.

Through coevolution, natural ecosystems (forests, rivers, oceans) have achieved *sustainability*, many with the lifespan of millions of years.

Controlling Complexity Is *NOT* Possible

Controlling complexity means attempting to make a complex system behave exactly as desired. The full control would mean restricting autonomy and connectivity of participants, in other words, destroying complexity and transforming a complex system into deterministic.

Autonomy, or the freedom of exercising choices in any social system, is limited by social conventions and norms, ethical standards, rules and regulations imposed by social system statutes and by national and international laws. Restrictions on the autonomy of individuals are normally enforceable by punishment, which can be severe (expulsion from a school, club, business; deportation from a country) or very severe (imprisonment, capital punishment).

In most cases, the motivation for limiting individual autonomy is reasonable, aimed at ensuring that the system (school, club, business, nation) behaves as closely as possible to what was intended.

However, if attempts are made to impose a full control on individuals (political dictatorship, military occupation), the social system will not be able to self-organise when hit by disruptive events, which in time will lead to disintegration (centrally planned economies have perished; military occupations, with some exceptions, have ended badly for the occupiers).

Also, the system is likely to resist the imposition of unreasonable control by creating an unofficial parallel social system (underground movement, guerrilla warfare) where dissidents are able to participate in prohibited activities (exchanging illegal books, discussing forbidden topics, planning or executing attacks). Unofficial, parallel social systems exhibit all the features of complexity, including self-organisation, which ensures its long-term success over the rigid control.

Even if controls are considered acceptable by the majority of members, opinions of some individuals and groups may differ on what the desirable autonomy should be, and some will practise what they believe, probably, in a covert manner (political dissent, infidelity, lying, theft, murder) or organise resistance aimed at changing the official order (rebellions, revolutions).

The idea that it is possible to control a social system by highly restricting the autonomy of constituent participants may be temporarily possible only if the system is closed to external influences. Such situations do not exist naturally but may occasionally be artificially imposed (Berlin Wall).

In a modern world, politicians who attempt to impose the absolute control on a nation sooner or later face the inevitable hurdle—controlling a nation is too complex a task for any individual (or a group of like-minded individuals). Sooner or later, mistakes are made, and dictatorship ends.

Managing Complexity

Managing complexity is a term that covers various ways of resolving issues created by increased complexity of the environment in which we live and work.

It is important to note that we can manage only those complex systems that we own, which we manage on behalf of owners or which we design. For example, a board of directors of a private company may decide that complexity of the company needs to be modified and may launch a complexity design project. And, of course, designers engaged in the design of complex adaptive software will deal all the time with the issue of how complex their software should be and how to achieve the desired level of complexity.

We cannot manage complexity of our environment which, by definition, is not under our control. There is nothing we can do about, for example, complexity of the current global political constellation.

What we can do is to match the complexity of organisations that operate in such an environment to the complexity of the environment.

Law of Requisite Complexity

The law of requisite complexity is the fundamental law of complexity management.

A system can survive and prosper only if its complexity is matched to the complexity of the environment in which it operates.

An alternative way of expressing the same idea would be:

If an organisation operates in a complex market, its complexity must match the complexity of the market.
If software supports a complex organisation, its complexity must match the complexity of the organisation.

Rigidly structured corporations and administrations, which were designed to operate in a stable, predictable environment, are currently exposed to increased complexity of the Internet-based global market and, therefore, must be *injected with requisite complexity* using appropriate digital tools—the process integral to *digital transformation*.

This clearly spells the end of the road for traditional deterministic software—in time, when most of the rigidly structured corporations are converted into adaptive enterprises, we shall use only *complex adaptive software*. Following the logic of the law of requisite complexity, deterministic software will not be able to support complex adaptive organisations.

Origins of the Law of Requisite Complexity

Back in 1956, in his book *An Introduction to Cybernetics*, Ashby stipulated a principle that later became the first law of cybernetics—*the law of requisite variety*—which stated that for a system to be stable, the number of states that its control mechanism is capable of attaining (its variety) must be greater than or equal to the number of states in the system being controlled.

For the purposes of his research, I have paraphrased Ashby's law and adapted it to a situation in which two complex systems interact. The term, the law of requisite complexity, is now common in literature on complexity, and my attempts to find out who was the first to publish it did not yield a reliable result.

Clustering

Clustering means partitioning a complex group into sparsely connected smaller groups of participants, as depicted on the right-hand side of Fig. 2.1.

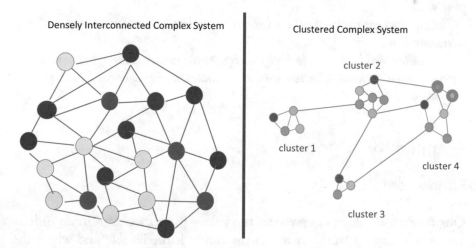

Fig. 2.1 Two contrasting configurations of complex systems

Clustering is of immense importance in managing complexity—it prevents, or at least reduces, negative consequences of butterfly effects, drifts into failure and extreme events such as a war and, at the same time, increases the effectiveness of the interaction between participants.

All living creatures live in small groups (clusters)—they self-organise into swarms, colonies, herds, packs, tribes, families, communities and nations. In a group where all participants know each other, it is easier to collectively create and distribute resources for life, grow and age together and experience a feeling of comfort and security.

A good example of clustering is the way in which recent immigrants to London self-organised themselves into cultural clusters—the French in

Kensington, the Indian in Southall, the Polish in Ealing and the Russians in Knightsbridge, to mention just a few.

Among biological systems, there are many examples of clustering. The human brain, a beautiful creation of natural selection, consists of connected regions (clusters), with each focusing on performing a particular function. For example, different regions of a human brain are engaged when people lie and when they are truthful.

Founded in 1096, the first English university, Oxford, was, and still is, organised as a system of connected colleges—each college being a cluster of intense educational activities where academics and students live and learn in relatively small groups. Cambridge, 100 years younger university, functions in the same way. Two examples of man-made clustered complex systems.

In contrast, modern universities are, as a rule, organised like corporations and run by administrators—a type of organisation that will straggle in a complex world.

Brexit is an example of voters preferring to live in a cluster—a traditional sovereign state.

We really should ask ourselves why we ignore the clustered configuration, which emerged from natural selection and is so successful in biological and natural ecosystems.

Complexity Science

Fundamentals

Our traditional education prepares the young to be successful in an orderly and slow-changing world in which the future is predictable and where the source of uncertainty is often ignorance and, therefore, can be reduced, or even eliminated, through learning. In such a *deterministic world*, according to Newton, natural laws are valid independently of time and location. Einstein asserted determinism by stating "God doesn't play dice with the universe".

As recently as the 1990s, a different worldview was articulated by the Belgian Nobel Prize winner, Ilya Prigogine [12, 13], and by the US Santa Fe Institute researcher, Stuart Kauffman [14, 15]—a *complexity worldview*. Many eminent authors have made important contributions to the idea of a complex evolving world, without necessarily mentioning the term complexity. Among them are Charles Darwin [16], Karl Popper [17] and Marvin Minsky [18]. Eric Beinhocker authored a comprehensive account of the complexity of the global market [19].

In sharp contrast to Einstein' assertion of determinism, Prigogine pro-claimed "Future is not given".

The idea is, of course, not entirely new; Heraclitus realised, as early as 500 BC, that the world is perpetually changing and expressed this notion in a memorable sentence "You could not step twice into the same river".

Karl Popper observed that in a deterministic world creativity would not be possible.

The *subject* of complexity science is the behaviour of complex systems, and the *method* is primarily experimental. Good results have been achieved by trial-and-error method.

Complexity Worldview

The essence of the complexity worldview is that *the world, far from being cre-ated to a great design, irreversibly and unpredictably evolves from early begin-nings, through the stage of primordial soup, to the current state, and will continue to evolve, driven by the accumulation of everyday actions and interactions of all living and non-living constituent components.* Every infection, war, scientific discovery, trading transaction, financial crisis, erosion, earthquake, tsunami, war, or procreation changes the world in a small and unpredictable way.

Uncertainty is a result of unpredictable evolution and cannot be eliminated.

If you perceive the world as perpetually evolving, time plays an important role. To discover evolutionary patterns, it is not sufficient to understand the current state; it is necessary to understand how we arrived to where we are now.

Complexity Mindset

Complexity mindset is a mindset which encompasses the complexity world-view, as explained above. Developing a complexity mindset is essential for those who live and work under conditions of complexity.

Which means for all of us.

The contrast between deterministic and complexity worldviews is illus-trated in Table 2.2.

The key difference is that the belief in determinism leads to the illusion that the future is, in principle, predictable and that we are in control of our life. And although, in practice, we find that the key elements of our future (health, wellbeing, security) are uncertain, determinism leads us to believe that uncer-tainty is caused by lack of knowledge and, therefore, in time, as we gain the required knowledge, we shall be able to predict the future.

Table 2.2 Deterministic and complexity worldviews

DETERMINISTIC WORLDVIEW	COMPLEX WORLDVIEW
World is created according to a "grand design".	World irreversibly and unpredictably evolves from early beginnings via primordial soup to a global village.
Future is predictable.	Future is not given.
There is universal law which predicts everything. We are waiting for it to be discovered.	Future emerges from billions of interactions among constituent agents, living and non-living, and is therefore not predictable.
Uncertainty = 0	0 < Uncertainty < 1
If we are uncertain, it is because of our lack of knowledge. Learning eliminates uncertainty.	Uncertainty is an inherent property of complexity and cannot be eliminated by learning.
Time and space are invariant.	"Becoming" is as important as "being".
For every effect, there is a cause.	Effects are triggered by reaching the tipping point due to the accumulation of many causes, which may be individually insignificant.
We can control behaviour of constituent systems of the world.	Our capacity to control complex systems is a delusion; we can only influence behaviour of our environment (natural or social) through coevolution.

Table 2.3 Worldviews of some of the intellectual giants throughout the centuries

DETERMINISTIC WORLDVIEW	COMPLEX WORLDVIEW
428 BC Plato Before you use energy to move matter you must have an **idea** why, what and how to move (idea = information, as an integral part of science).	564 BC Buddha Mind is the forerunner of all things; all phenomena are mind-made (from the Dhammapada).
384 BC Aristotle The world consists of matter and energy (information was ignored).	535 BC Heraclitus You could not step twice into the same river.
1643 Newton Natural laws are valid at any time and at any location.	1831 James Clerk Maxwell Wrote about a new kind of knowledge that would overcome the prejudice of determinism.
1879 Einstein God doesn't play dice with universe. Time is an illusion.	1902 Karl Popper In a deterministic world it would be impossible to choose or create.
	1917 Prigogine – father of Complexity The end of certainty. Future is not given.

The main consequence of believing that the world is complex is the understanding that the future is, in principle, unpredictable. It teaches us that the uncertainty is an inherent property of the world which, in some cases, can be reduced by relevant information, but it cannot be removed entirely. It leads us to study how to manage complexity—how to adapt to unpredictable changes, how to resist unpredictable attacks and how to coevolve with our everchanging socioeconomic environment.

Since the world is complex, rather than random, the evolution follows *discernible patterns*. Therefore, although the future is not given, we may determine the likelihood of certain scenarios.

Pattern recognition is the most important skill for those who live under conditions of complexity.

Both deterministic and complex worldviews coexisted through centuries. Even the ancient Greek civilisation embraced one eminent complexity thinker—Heraclitus. However, determinism dominated and is probably still the prevailing worldview. The twenty-first century will be the turning point (Table 2.3).

Key Points

1. Every important aspect of the twenty-first-century world is *complex*, including global political constellation, religious conflicts, military conflicts, the Internet-based global market, mass migration and epidemics.
2. Some of the salient features of complex systems are:

   - Their global behaviour *emerges* from the *interaction* of participants—it cannot be deduced by studying individual participants—and is unpredictable but not random.
   - Complex systems are capable of *self-organising* (or even mutating) to *adapt* to any disruption or attack—therefore, they are perpetually changing.
   - Global complex systems *cannot be controlled*—they can be only, possibly, influenced.

3. Politicians, clergy, military experts, economists, administrators, epidemiologists and many other "specialists" (in their narrow subjects) attempt to resolve complex issues *without understanding key feature of complexity*, often with disastrous consequences.
4. To resolve negative issues created by the recent sharp rise in complexity, we need to cultivate the *natural intelligence* of world population and develop the *artificial intelligence* of digital systems.

References

1. Rzevski, G., P. Skobelev, "Managing Complexity". WIT Press, Southampton, Boston, 2014. ISBN 978-1-84564-936-4.
2. Rzevski, G. "Coevolution of Technology, Business and Society", International Journal of Design & Nature and Ecodynamics, Volume 13 No. 3 (2018), pp. 231-237. ISSN: 1755-7437.
3. Rzevski, G. "Managing Complexity: Theory and Practice". 11th System of Systems Engineering Conference (SoSE), 12-16 June 2016, Kongsberg, Norway, pp. 1-6.

4. Rzevski, G., "Complexity as the Defining Feature of the 21st Century". International Journal of Design & Nature and Ecodynamics. Volume 10, No 3 (2015), pp. 191-198. ISSN: 1755-7437.
5. Gleick, J., "Chaos: Making a New Science", Heinemann, 1988.
6. Taleb, N., "The Black Swan: The Impact of the Highly Improbable". Penguin Books, 2007.
7. Dekker, S., "Drift into failure: from hunting broken components to understanding complex systems", Ashgate, Farnham, 2011, ISBN 978-1-4094-2222-8.
8. Rzevski, G., "Using Tools of Complexity Science to Diagnose the Current Financial Crisis". Optoelectronics, Instrumentation and Data Processing, Vol. 46 (2010), No. 2. ISSN 8756-6990.
9. Rzevski, G., Skobelev, P., "Emergent Intelligence in Large Scale Multi-Agent Systems". International Journal of Education and Information Technology, Issue 2, Volume 1 (2007), pp. 64-71.
10. Rzevski, G. "Harnessing the Power of Self-Organisation" International Journal of Design & Nature and Ecodynamics, Volume 11 No 4 (2016), pp. 483-494. ISSN: 1755-7437.
11. Rzevski, G. "Self-Organisation in Social Systems". Ontology of Designing. N 4 (14), pp. 8-17, 2014. ISSN 2223-9537.
12. Prigogine, Ilya, "The End of Certainty: Time, Chaos and the new Laws of Nature". Free Press, 1997.
13. Prigogine, Ilya, "Is Future Given?" World Scientific Publishing Co., 2003.
14. Kaufman, S., "At Home In the Universe: The Search for the Laws of Self-Organization and Complexity". Oxford University Press, 1995.
15. Kaufman, S., "A World Beyond Physics: The Emergence and Evolution of Life". Oxford University Press, 2019. ISBN-13: 978-0190871338.
16. Darwin, C., "On the Origin of Species by Means of Natural Selection". London: John Murray, 1859.
17. Popper, K., "Conjectures and Refutations: The Growth of Scientific Knowledge". Rutledge & Kegan Paul Ltd, London (1963).
18. Minsky, M., "The Society of Mind". Heinemann, 1985. ISBN 0 434 46758 8
19. Beinhocker, Eric, "The Origin of Wealth: Evolution, Complexity and the Radical Remaking of Economics". Random House Business Books, 2007.

3

Artificial Intelligence: Friend or Foe

Introduction

Globalisation and the widespread use of digital communication technology have increased the *connectivity* and, consequently, *complexity* of our socioeconomic environment. And complexity creates *uncertainty*.

The case in point is the Internet-based global market in which many millions or, possibly, billions of concurrent participants create, modify or cancel transactions with an unprecedented speed, making forecasting of supply and demand next to impossible.

However, the behaviour of complex systems, such as the Internet-based global market, although unpredictable, is not random; it follows discernible *patterns*; and an effective pattern recognition tool is *intelligence*—natural or artificial.

Artificial intelligence is particularly good at recognising patterns which are hidden in a mass of data (e.g. diagnosing cancers or identifying trends in demand) and where the speed of identifying consequences of a disruptive event is of great importance (e.g. identifying which part of a healthcare process will have to be rescheduled in order to eliminate, or at least reduce, consequences of an unexpected change of a medical procedure).

Recent commercial success of many AI systems and, in particular, the so-called generative AI, as represented by *chatbots* (ChatGPT, Bard), sparked a plethora of articles exaggerating the power of AI or warning us of its imagined dangers. There is even a motion to slow down AI development by introducing an international moratorium on all advanced AI research for at least 6 months. I wonder how would that help? What would be different in 6-month time?

G. Rzevski, *The Future is Digital*, https://doi.org/10.1007/978-3-031-37810-2_3

What Is Intelligence?

There is no generally agreed definition of intelligence. It is a complex concept that includes, for example, the capacity for abstraction, logic, understanding, self-awareness, learning, reasoning, planning, creativity, critical thinking, problem-solving and organising information into an easily accessible knowledge framework.

Cambridge dictionary defines intelligence as "the ability to understand and learn well, and to form judgements and opinions based on reason".

The psychologist Robert Sternberg defined intelligence as "mental activity directed toward purposive adaptation to, selection, and shaping of real-world environments relevant to one's life".

The implication is that before we can start with adaptation to and shaping of anything, we must select what to do and how to do it; in other words, we must *make decisions*.

The notion is not new; as early as 400 BC, Plato wrote that before applying energy to move matter, one must have an *idea* what, where and how to move it, which implies collecting and processing relevant information and making decisions.

Since "purposive adaptation to, selection, and shaping of real-world environments relevant to one's life" is a complex behaviour resulting in an uncertain outcome, we can deduce that *an important aspect of intelligence is the ability to make effective decisions under conditions of uncertainty* [1].

The human brain seems to have a natural ability to find order in chaos. According to designers of the IQ test, *pattern recognition is a key determinant of a person's intelligence*. The ability to find patterns is important for survival and prosperity in a complex environment—it enables us to recognise potential threats and opportunities.

Another aspect of intelligence, particularly important for those who have to cope with uncertainty and ambiguity of a complex socioeconomic environment, is the ability to hold in one's mind several competing ideas and accepting that there are questions which cannot be answered by binary answers such as yes/no, guilty/not guilty or correct/incorrect.

Human Brain

The human brain is an immensely complex system. It consists of about 100 billion neurons (brain cells) and about 1000 trillion synaptic interconnections between neurons. Each neuron may be connected to up to 1000 other neurons forming a formidably complex natural *neural network* [2]. It is important to note that every cell has a copy of the *human genome*, which guides neural network growth, operation and evolution. Humans are not born as "blank slates" (tabula rasa). Babies are born with a pre-wired, small neural network to enable them to perform basic functions, such as finding, consuming and processing food. There is no need to train them how to survive when they emerge into the unknown world [3].

As human offsprings grow, the complexity of their neural networks develops in interaction with the environment, and their intellectual capabilities increase as their neural network grows [4].

Scientists at the University College London (UCL) have discovered recently that two hemispheres of the human brain are differently wired [5]. The right-hand hemisphere has different synapses—connections between neurons—which enable the easier creation of new network configurations and therefore facilitate creative behaviour. The left-hand hemisphere has stronger connections between neurons and is responsible for human features that rarely need to change such as logical thinking and linguistic fluency.

Although the notion that each brain hemisphere has a different specialised function is disputed by other researchers, the UCL finding *that a difference in neuron wiring leads to different behaviour* is significant.

I have discovered the same principle by experimenting with the strength of connections between digital neurons, which helped me to design different kinds of digital neural network behaviour by adjusting the type of wiring of digital neurons. Learning from UCL colleagues that the evolution arrived at the same principle was obviously valuable.

The importance of the human brain is illustrated by the allocation of resources which support its functions. Although the human brain represents only 2% of the body weight, it receives 15% of the cardiac output, 20% of the total body oxygen consumption and 25% of the total body glucose utilisation [6].

No single brain cell, or a group of cells, can be described as intelligent, and yet, the neural network, as a whole, exhibits all aspects of human intelligence. It follows that intelligence *emerges* from the interaction of neurons or, in other words, *human intelligence is an emergent property of the human brain.*

Artificial Intelligence

In 1950, English mathematician Alan Turing published a paper entitled "Computing Machinery and Intelligence" which was the first publication on how to build digital systems that exhibit intelligence.

In 1955, Stanford professor John McCarthy coined the term *artificial intelligence*, defined by him as "the science and engineering of making intelligent machines".

The name artificial intelligence (AI) is now universally adopted. The alternative and probably more appropriate term would be *digital intelligence*.

As the scientific field of artificial intelligence has developed, every new variant was given a new name—*artificial neural networks, machine learning, deep learning* and *emergent intelligence* [7].

A significant difference, however, exists only between two types of AI systems.

Systems which consist of an artificial neural network as "clean slate", which have to be trained to exhibit intelligence

Systems which, like the human brain, have pre-stored knowledge, represented as a semantic network (ontology), enabling the system to exhibit intelligence without being trained

AI which must be trained before it can perform will be called here *machine learning*.

AI which contains pre-stored knowledge and does not need to be trained is called here *emergent AI*.

Machine Learning

Artificial neural networks, on which machine learning is based, are at present rather simplistic imitations of natural neural networks. They may have up to 1000 neurons, whilst the brain has 100 billion. There is no equivalent of a genome, and therefore, there is no knowledge to guide their development and behaviour—consequently, neither self-organisation nor evolution is possible.

Because artificial neural networks must be trained to function, their performance critically depends on the quality of data used for training. This doesn't seem to be a big problem because digital technology excels in capturing and storing data.

Well-trained artificial neural networks are *very powerful tools for solving a wide variety of narrowly specialised complex problems*.

A distinct class of machine learning is *generative AI*, which can be trained to create new documents, essays, poems, images, videos and musical compositions. Their answers to user's questions always sound plausible but may be wrong.

Emergent AI

Emergent AI is a network of short algorithms, called *agents* (equivalent of neurons or groups of neurons), supported by *ontology* (equivalent of the human genome). Emergent AI, like the human brain, has the capacity for creating *emergent intelligence* [8, 9].

Agents can compete or cooperate with each other; they can negotiate deals, resolve conflicts and have certain autonomy in choosing how to behave. Emergent AI has all powerful features of complex systems—it can *self-organise to adapt, repel attacks, improve own performance, perform "creative destruction" and coevolve with its environment.*

At the present level of development, emergent AI is especially good at making rapid, consistent and precise decisions *under conditions of low to moderate uncertainty.* For example, it has been successfully used for managing supply chains.

Differences Between Human and Artificial Intelligence

Differences between human intelligence (HI) and artificial intelligence (AI) are summarised in Table 3.1.

Table 3.1 Essential differences between human and artificial intelligence

TYPE OF INTELLIGENCE	FEATURES
Emergent human intelligence	Every brain cell has a copy of the human genome.
	Children are born with the pre-wired knowledge.
	Human neural networks grow in interaction with the environment, guided by genes.
	Each half of the brain is differently wired.
	Neurons have a very high connectivity – estimated value of 1,000.
	Human brain has 100 billion brain cells.
Emergent artificial intelligence	Ontology takes the role of the genome.
	Agents act as neurons, or clusters of neurons.
	Strength of links between agents may be adjusted to increase/decrease complexity.
	Agent networks are adaptive.
	Agents have connectivity of the order of 100.
	Emergent AI has, typically, 100,000 – 500,000 agents.
	Agent networks are capable of selforganising and coevolving with their environment and exhibit emergent properties.
Machine learning	Artificial neural networks are tabula rasa (clean slates).
	Must be trained on large sets of data.
	If data is inadequate, the performance of the network will be deficient.
	Artificial neural networks are static, they don't grow or evolve.
	Generative AI can create documents, essays, poems, images, videos and music.

Division of Labour Between Human and Artificial Intelligence

Current AI systems have a limited intelligence, and it will take many years of intensive development for these systems to be able to meaningfully compete with very intelligent humans.

Complex activities, requiring creativity, imagination, vision and the ability to manage high risks in a variety of circumstances, will be performed by humans for some time, if not forever. Highly intelligent scientific researchers, jet engine designers, medical consultants, philosophers, top novelists and musicians and entrepreneurs should not lose sleep over AI—any type of AI.

However, in business, administration, education, healthcare, defence and everyday life, there are many activities that can be effectively performed by AI systems of limited intelligence far better than by HI:

Low-risk, operational activities, such as scheduling of human, physical and financial resources for manufacturing, retail, education, healthcare services, defence and many others

Creating documents and images and handling correspondence

Narrowly specialised activities, such as diagnosing a health problem, pre-selecting applicants for a job, testing students, fulfilling online orders (Amazon has to package 50,000 orders per hour), interpreting images received from drones, navigating driverless vehicles, conducting conversation with online users, extracting knowledge on the behaviour of an organisation from the data on its operation collected over a long period of time and many others

AI systems can make decisions on the allocation of resources at high speed and precision 24 h a day and are more effective and less expensive than human operatives currently performing these tasks. In the near future, AI systems will be employed to manage operational activities on an unprecedented scale. Human intelligence will not be able to compete with artificial intelligence at this level.

Replacing 40% of human decision-makers with the emergent artificial intelligence could create a *high-tech, high-wage, high-productivity economy* and, at the same time, solve the current problem of workforce shortages.

Savings achieved by AI could be directed into the creation of new employment opportunities requiring skills in *leading, motivating, encouraging, caring, comforting, supporting and maintaining*, which are outside the reach of AI, at least, at present. These new jobs would greatly improve levels of customer support in all service industries and particularly in healthcare.

We just have to accept that there will be a considerable shift in employment opportunities for humans when AI takes over making decisions under the conditions of low uncertainty or narrow specialisation.

Table 3.2 Human and artificial intelligence—division of labour

REQUIREMENTS	HUMAN INTELLIGENCE	ARTIFICIAL INTELLIGENCE
High cognitive intelligence	Researchers, strategists, philosophers, designers of complex and complicated systems, medical experts, defence thinkers.	
High social (emotional) intelligence	Team coordinators, politicians, customer service providers, marketing and sales executives, nurses, carers, tutors.	
High artistic intelligence	Architects, interior decorators, painters, composers, novelists, script writers, film directors, actors, graphic designers, furniture designers, fashion designers, landscape designers.	
High money-making intelligence	Investors, bankers, entrepreneurs.	
High dexterity	Plumbers, electricians, builders, decorators; footballers.	
Moderate creative intelligence	All human beings can perform such tasks.	Chatbots are competent and often better than humans in writing documents, essays and answers to emails; generating simple poems and simple novels; creating images, composing music and corresponding with people using natural language.
Moderate intelligence, low risk decisions, high speed & precision, working 24 hours a day (40% of all jobs in business).		The allocation of resources to demands, production, supply chains, deliveries, warehousing, purchasing, transport (road transport, airlines, railways, containers, tankers, ambulances, multi-mode transport), health care (appointments, beds, operating theatres, human resources), travel, tourism, water supply.
High intelligence applied to specific problems/		Extracting knowledge from data (analytics), diagnosing, driving.

Human Versus Artificial Intelligence: Competing or Collaborating?

Table 3.2 shows that there are few areas where *competition* between HI and AI is feasible or useful [10]. The exceptions are tasks requiring moderate creative intelligence, such as generating standard documents, essays, images, videos and music, which can be performed either by humans or chatbots.

On the other hand, *collaboration* between human and artificial intelligence is not only feasible but highly desirable. Consider a business where operational decisions are performed by AI systems and strategic decisions by human executives—knowledge workers. In such situations, we would expect HI to set targets for AI, monitor its decision-making using appropriate displays and analyse its performance with a view to introducing corrections, if required. AI systems would consult executives whenever their domain knowledge is inadequate.

Is AI Dangerous?

Considering that human intelligence is occasionally used for committing fraudulent or criminal activities and for domination and that intelligent people make mistakes, it is not surprising that artificial intelligence could be employed for shady purposes and that it could blunder.

Using AI for fraud and criminal activities is a growing business, and as the power of AI systems increases, its fraudulent and criminal usage will rise. Examples include impersonating a victim, removing money from accounts, hacking and similar. Generative AI is massively used for forging essays, homework, CVs and similar documents. And, of course, chatbots can be silly or dangerously wrong.

However, with the help of superior HI or AI, it is easy to find out if a document (say, homework) was written by a person or a chatbot.

Can AI Dominate the Human Race?

Serious concerns have been raised about a possibility for AI systems to develop intelligence superior to that of humans; to jump to the top of dominance hierarchy, occupied at present by humans; and to enslave us.

Let's consider this possibility.

Human intelligence is an emergent property of the human brain, which has around 100 billion neurons, each containing a copy of the human genome (with a huge amount of knowledge how neurons should behave) and ready to be connected into a gigantic network, which also contains sensors (detecting images, sound, smell, pressure) that enable the neural network to receive information from the external world. The human brain is connected to actuators (muscles), to act upon its decisions (push, pool, hit, press, touch, click, kiss).

Humans are born with a small pre-wired neural network, which is capable of self-organising to adapt and defend itself, learning, remembering, creating abstract and physical objects, solving problems under conditions of uncertainty, interacting with the external world and *growing* until it reaches its zenith and then declines.

Above all, the human brain is a biological system capable of absorbing energy that it needs from its environment.

Can we hope to construct from silicon such a wonderful intelligent machine? I doubt it.

In comparison, the artificial neural networks are minuscule (in terms of numbers of connections between neurons) and do not contain any knowledge comparable to the human genome—they must be trained using large amount of data to solve only a narrow range of problems.

Emergent AI systems are much closer in their organisation to the human brain. Nevertheless, with only hundreds of thousands of digital agents engaged in the exchange of messages, they cannot be compared with the brain capacity for growing a network of billions of interacting neurons with trillions of connections.

And, of course, since artificial intelligence systems are physical, rather than biological, it is possible to stop them by switching off electricity if we don't like what they do.

What Is the Risk of AI Making a Genuine Mistake?

Intelligence is applied when there is a need for making decisions under conditions of uncertainty. Under such conditions, any intelligence—human or artificial—is prone to making mistakes. Since this is a fact (rather than opinion), should we not start thinking how to prevent AI from making decisions which could result in a mistake endangering human life or wellbeing?

Consider driving under bad weather conditions on a narrow country road—a high-risk activity in which human life is at stake. Should responsibility for safely reaching the intended destination be handed over to the self-driving car or retained by the human driver?

My vote is for banning AI from making high-risk decisions whose outcomes may result in danger to humans. Instead, AI should be used to support human high-risk decision-makers with a good advice and by preventing humans committing mistakes that place them, or others, in danger.

Assigning Responsibility for Unethical AI Behaviour

We must agree, as soon as possible, who will be responsible for unethical AI behaviour and how to deal with them.

The two articles that appear on the same day in *The Times* (25th of May 2023) tell the complete story. One is entitled "AI has enabled a paralysed patient to walk again" and the other "Conman uses AI to pose as friend seeking £500,000".

Clearly, the culprits are people who use AI, or, even worse, train AI, to intentionally carry out criminal activities.

Not the technology.

Key Points

1. Intelligence, natural or artificial, has the capability of discovering patterns in the behaviour of complex systems and is a priceless tool for resolving issues created by complexity.
2. Human intelligence (HI) is superior in resolving high-risk strategic issues, in which understanding of the broad context of the issue is paramount.
3. Artificial intelligence (AI) is superior in:

   • Resolving low-risk operational issues, in which precision and speed of decision-making are essential
   • Solving important narrowly specialised complex problems—such as diagnosing cancer or extracting knowledge from large quantity of operational data (business analytics)

4. The human brain is an enormously complex thinking machine, able to comprehend a broad context of any practical problem. It is difficult to see how we could possibly construct an artificial intelligence system of similar power.
5. A widespread use of AI could replace an estimated 40% of low-risk and narrowly specialised decision-makers and create *a high-tech, high-wage, high-productivity economy.*
6. If the success of the industrial economy can be explained by the automation of production, in other words, *using industrial machines for performing manual work*, the success of the digital economy will be ensured by using AI to make low-risk decisions or, in other words, *using digital machines for performing intellectual work.*

References

1. Rzevski, G., P. Skobelev, "Managing Complexity". WIT Press, Southampton, Boston, 2014. ISBN 978-1-84564-936-4.
2. Edelman, G., "Bright Air. Brilliant Fire. On the Matter of the Mind". Allen Lane the Penguin Press, London, 1992.
3. Pinker, S., "The Blank Slate: The Modern Denial of Human Nature". Allen Lane, 2002. 0713992565.
4. Posner, M. I., & Rothbart, M. K. (2007). "Educating the human brain". American Psychological Association. https://doi.org/10.1037/11519-000.
5. ScienceDaily, "Neurons Hard Wired to Tell Left from Right", 2008.
6. BrainFacts.org, How Much Energy Does the Brain Use? 2019.
7. Patterson, J., A. Gibson "Deep Learning: A Practitioner's Approach", Google Books, 2017.
8. Rzevski, G., P. Skobelev, "Emergent Intelligence in Large Scale Multi-Agent Systems". International Journal of Education and Information Technology, Issue 2, Volume 1 (2007), pp. 64-71.
9. Rzevski, G.; Skobelev, P.; Zhilyaev, A. "Emergent Intelligence in Smart Ecosystems: Conflicts Resolution by Reaching Consensus in Resource Management". Mathematics 2022, 10, 1923. https://doi.org/10.3390/math10111923.
10. Rzevski, G., "Human versus Artificial Intelligence: Cooperating or Competing?". Keynote presentation at International Conference on Artificial Intelligence 2018, Colombo, Sri Lanka.

4

Natural and Digital Ecosystems

Introduction

Natural ecosystems, such as forests, grasslands, deserts, rivers and oceans, have a remarkable ability to *self-organise* in order to *adapt* to the changes, display *resilience* to attacks and *coevolve* with their environment, enabling some of them to *sustain* their existence for million years.

Can we design businesses, administrations, political organisations and cities to be adaptive, resilient and sustainable? And last long?

It is obvious that adaptive, resilient and sustainable businesses and administrations would be much more effective under new complex market conditions, just like natural ecosystems within their complex environment.

Many cities evolved into overcrowded, polluted conurbations chocked by traffic. By transforming them into smart urban ecosystems in which all services are adaptive, resilient and sustainable, we could improve life of both citizens and visitors.

The time has come to carefully look at natural ecosystems, which coped for centuries with the complexity and unpredictability of the natural world, and learn.

What Are Natural Ecosystems?

Our planet consists of a very large number of interconnected complex geographical clusters of living species and non-living elements—animals, plants, insects, microorganisms, soil, water, air and sunlight—called natural

G. Rzevski, *The Future is Digital*, https://doi.org/10.1007/978-3-031-37810-2_4

ecosystems. Examples include deserts, rivers, forests, seas, plains, grasslands, lakes and puddles.

Natural ecosystem components—agents—are linked by flows of information (messages carried by voices, noises, odours, chemicals), energy (photosynthesis, agents eating agents) and matter (nutrients).

Ecosystems operate like free markets—there is no central control. Participants compete or cooperate with each other depending on circumstances. The overall behaviour emerges from the interaction of constituent elements.

Let's look at a forest as a natural ecosystem in more details. Forest consists of interacting living organisms—mammals, birds, insects, flowers, moss and microorganisms—and the non-living elements such as soil, air and water. Forest ecosystems, without being centrally controlled, can survive fires, infections and all kinds of disruptive events and continue to exist for very long periods of time. This remarkable sustainability can be explained, in terms of complexity science, by their capacity for adapting to, and coevolving with, their environment, helped by the *competition and cooperation* of constituent living and non-living agents.

Animals manage the access to a water puddle on a forest clearance carefully attempting to avoid running into a hungry specimen of a species belonging to a higher level of *dominance hierarchy*. The process is a genuine adaptation—animals monitor signals transmitted by smell and noise, interpret received information and schedule/reschedule their actions in real time, based on the updated signals.

Plants communicate with each other through the air, by releasing odorous chemicals, and through the soil, by secreting soluble chemicals and transporting them along thread-like networks formed by soil fungi. The purpose of plant-to-plant messaging is usually to warn neighbours of the attack by insects [1]. A wonderful example of cooperation through the exchange of information.

From the above discussions and examples, it is clear that natural ecosystems are complex systems—they consist of a large number of diverse, partially autonomous, richly interconnected components, which cooperate or compete with each other without any central control and whose behaviour emerges from their interactions and is therefore uncertain (non-deterministic) without being random. It follows distinct patterns [2] (big cats feed on weaker animals such as antelopes).

What Are Digital Ecosystems?

Because the important elements of all artificial ecosystems are digital, man-made ecosystems are generally called *digital ecosystems*.

The trend to transform businesses into digital ecosystems began as early as 1993, triggered by the James Moore's article in Harvard Review [3]. The process is known as *digital transformation*.

Digital transformation is a popular name for using advanced digital technology to replace outdated practices and technologies. Initially, the emphasis was on the use of software packages and on data technologies—big data and clouds. Artificial intelligence (of machine learning variety) was included later and used primarily for analytics (extraction of knowledge from data).

It is now time to rethink the whole concept.

To be really smart, digital transformation must focus on *building adaptability, resilience and sustainability into traditional businesses and administrations* [2].

Organisations experiencing volatile demand for their products or services will be the first in the queue for smart digital transformation. Rigid enterprise resource planning (ERP) systems are not cost-effective when demands cannot be predicted. They will be replaced with systems capable of instantly detecting unpredictable changes in demand or supply, rapidly assessing the impact of the disruption and rescheduling resources to neutralise the disruption before the next disruptive event occurs.

This objective can be achieved by injecting artificial intelligence into key business processes.

At the operational level: AI-based real-time schedulers, real-time project management systems and generative AI for creating documents and handling correspondence, particularly, email systems

At the tactical/strategic level: AI-based, real-time decision support systems

Here are some examples of operational business processes that can be cost-effectively performed by AI: management of supply chains, production, purchasing, transport and payments of invoices; the allocation of working capital to organisational units and projects; and project management.

At tactical and strategic levels: AI-based systems are superior to traditional software packages in many applications, including analytics for customer relations, marketing, forecasting of demand and monitoring of competition; long-term planning of capacity for supply chains, production, purchasing and transport; and evaluation of options when designing supply chains, marketing campaigns, acquisitions and expansions.

And finally, emerging AI technology will be used for designing the enterprise knowledge base, which contains all polices, rules, regulations and best practices necessary for effectively running the business and is both computer readable and accessible to employees.

To understand how to transform a traditional organisation into a digital ecosystem, let's re-examine the concept of *organisation*.

Organisation as a System of Resources

In essence, an organisation is a system of resources—*human, financial, physical and knowledge resources*—assembled to perform a *set of tasks* within a specific *demand-supply environment* and with a view to achieving a set of goals.

If the goal is to provide income, the environment is economic, and the organisation is a business.

If the goal is to provide decision-making support for politicians, the environment is political, and the organisation is an administration.

If the goal is to prepare for life, the environment is education, and the organisation is a training unit, a school, a college or a university.

If the goal is to maintain our mind and body in good order, the environment is a healthcare market, and the organisation is a healthcare unit.

If the goal is to defend a nation, the environment is military, and the organisation is a defence unit.

In traditional organisations, lines of command and reporting are well defined, business processes are precisely specified, and tasks are planned well in advance. Such organisations are supposed to behave in a predictable way and to deliver results in stable markets.

Organisation as a Complex System

To make organisations resemble natural ecosystems, in other words, to make them adaptive, resilient and sustainable, we must design organisations to be *complex*, which means to eliminate, or at least reduce, centralised control and enable organisational resources to *interact* with each other by exchanging messages.

The first thing is to empower human resources to use their intelligence and participate in decision-making by exchanging messages with each other.

To enable non-living resources to exchange messages, we must build an intelligent *digital twin* of the organisation in which each real organisational resource is represented by a *digital agent*. The occurrence of a disruptive event in the real world is then instantly conveyed to the digital twin, which rapidly reschedules resources to neutralise or, at least, reduce negative consequences of the disruption and send the new schedules to its *real twin*.

With the help of a digital twin, the matching complexity of an organisation to complexity of its environment—remember the law of requisite complexity—is done by *matching the speed of scheduling and rescheduling of resources to the frequency of disruptive events*.

At the strategic levels, human intelligence will dominate artificial intelligence for a very long period, possibly forever. The broad understanding of the world in which we live and work, necessary for developing the strategy for maintaining adaptability and sustainability, is at present beyond artificial intelligence.

To be adaptive at the strategic level, it is necessary for decision-makers to widen the scope of deliberations to be able to *anticipate* new, complexity-induced patterns in supply and demand, which is best done as a teamwork by participants with diverse knowledge profiles.

The adaptive strategy requires teams of strategists to:

Monitor social, economic and political trends relevant to the environment in which the enterprise operates

Analyse possible consequences of identified trends

Review the strategy of the enterprise, based on analytical results

To summarise, because of the requirement for faster decision-making at lower levels and wider understanding of the rapidly changing big picture at higher levels of management, the traditional hierarchical management structures are not suitable for operation under conditions of complexity.

Distributed decision-making—the interconnected clusters of decision-makers, with each cluster working on a well-defined problem—is the model for the future.

And how do we make organisations resilient?

The process of making an organisation resilient is the same as the process of making it adaptive. The difference is in which data to monitor and what to look for. To achieve adaptability, we monitor the flow of orders and behaviour of resources, and for resilience, we are trying to spot unexpected deviations from normal behaviour of both the organisation as a whole and of each of its members.

A section of a digital system which protects the system from attacks and fraud may be called a *smart digital immunity system*.

A smart digital immunity system protects organisations from electronic attacks and fraud and builds resilience into organisations by:

Continuously monitoring all the relevant data streams and databases and instantly detecting a deviation from normal behaviour, probably due to an attack or fraud

Performing a quick analysis to assess the consequences and to check if the unexpected behaviour is an attack, a fraud or a random disturbance

Rescheduling the relevant resources to foil the attack or fraud without disturbing unaffected parts of the system, if possible

Protecting organisations from drift into failure is not much different. However, it includes continuously monitoring activities of participants and, therefore, may interfere with privacy. The aim is to detect human errors or illegal activities, which although insignificant by themselves, if undetected, may accumulate and reach the tipping point.

Coevolution of a complex system and its complex environment results in sustainable systems which are always "in tune" with their environment. To achieve sustainability, it is sufficient to ensure that the complexity of a system is matched with the complexity of the environment.

Virtual Organisation

A *virtual organisation* is a network of organisational units or individuals, each possibly at a different location, working together on a project. Participants are free to connect to other networks when desirable or required [4].

What Are Smart Digital Ecosystems?

Smart digital ecosystems are open, adaptive, resilient and sustainable socio-technological organisations, consisting of interacting participants, which could be human and/or digital agents, that compete or cooperate with each other without being centrally controlled.

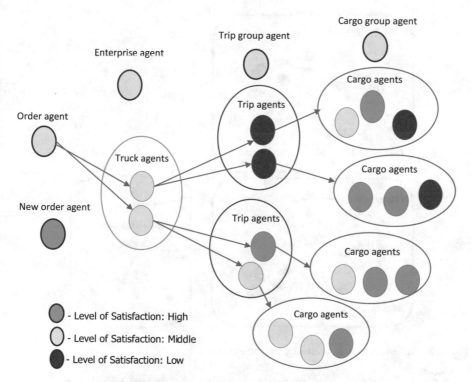

Fig. 4.1 Smart digital ecosystem architecture

The architecture and the method for designing smart digital ecosystems presented in this book are to the best of my knowledge original and very practical [5].

As Fig. 4.1 shows, a smart digital ecosystem contains three key subsystems: *real world, digital twin* and *knowledge base* (ontology + data).

Real world consists of demands (orders) and resources (human, physical and financial).

Digital twin is a one-to-one replica of the resources of the real organisation to which it is connected. It consists of intensely interacting digital agents (short algorithms), primarily *demand agents,* representing real demands, and *resource agents*, representing real resources.

Agents are the decision-makers, and they arrive at decisions through a process of negotiation among themselves and, occasionally, involving human decision-makers (Fig. 4.2).

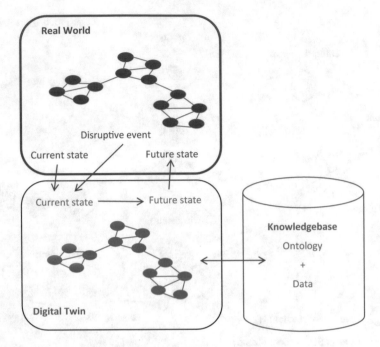

Fig. 4.2 Agents make decisions by negotiation

Digital agents have emotions—they can be satisfied with their schedule or not. Agents with a lower level of satisfaction may initiate rescheduling.

Other emotions may be introduced such as fear, say, from high-risk decisions.

Here is how a real organisation and its digital twin work together.

When an unpredictable disruptive event occurs in the real world, digital agents, resident in the digital twin, rapidly detect the disruption; identify parts of the real world that will be affected; reschedule the affected resources, without disrupting the operation of the unaffected parts of the system; and send instruction to the real world on how to neutralise the disruption. All this is done in real time, often in seconds or even microseconds.

Knowledge base (ontology + data) contains the domain knowledge required to run the ecosystem. It consists of two distinctive parts: *ontology*, which contains conceptual knowledge organised as a semantic network, and *data*.

Ontology can be updated whenever rules, regulations or policies of the organisation change, without interrupting the smart digital ecosystem operation.

In large smart digital ecosystems, the digital twin may consist of several *swarms* of digital agents, each allocating resources to demands for a different product or service.

Practical Applications of Smart Digital Ecosystems

For more than 20 years, with a team of co-workers, I have designed and build for commercial clients around the world large-scale emergent AI systems, which exhibit adaptability, resilience and spontaneous self-improvement.
Examples include:

Real-time scheduler for 2000 minicabs in London [6]
Real-time scheduler for the distribution of Coca-Cola bottles across Germany
Real-time scheduler for managing 10% of world capacity of large seagoing tankers transporting crude oil from the Middle East to the North America
A swarm of real-time schedulers delivering cargo to the International Space Station [7]
Complex adaptive data and text mining system for insurers [8]
AI-based digital translator from Singhalese to English [9]
AI-based semantic processor for reading scientific abstracts for a client in the USA
Real-time scheduler for LEGO [10]
Real-time scheduler for one of the largest car rental companies in the world [11]
Real-time scheduler for an aircraft manufacturer [12]
AI-based controller for the ventilation, cooling and heating of a large building in subtropical regions for a client in Florida
Real-time scheduler for railways [13]
Smart city

Let's look at some of these systems.

Case Study 1: Smart City

Let us consider a typical urban settlement governed by the council and managed by the town administration responsible for services to citizens, such as education, social services, roads and transport, waste disposal, economic development, planning, protecting the public (from crime, fire, elements, etc.), libraries, rubbish collection, environmental health, tourism, leisure and amenities, housing needs services and collection of council tax.

And let's assume that the council has decided to substantially improve each service to citizens and at the same time reduce the costs of service provision.

The above services may be delivered by the town administration or out-sourced to private companies, in which case we would deal with an ecosystem containing both public and private sectors.

Requirements Specification

The conventional wisdom is to approach the problem top-down by attempting to perform a requirements specification for the whole town before starting the work on design.

Such approach would be unacceptable under current dynamics of the political, social, economic and technological town environment. The dynamics is such that the requirements would be obsolete before completed.

An evolutionary design method is advocated by the author, as described below.

Consider all services with a view to identifying one whose improvement would bring the highest value to the client.

Complete a requirements specification for the improvement of the selected service.

Design a part of a digital ecosystem consisting of the selected service only.

Evaluate and update the solution demonstrating the achieved increase in the client value.

Select the next service and repeat the previous steps ensuring that the newly added service cooperates or competes with the previously improved services, as required.

As the number of improved services increases, continuously monitor and, if necessary, adjust the overall ecosystem design.

In theory, the evolutionary improvement of services should never stop. In practice, contractual arrangements between clients and smart digital ecosystem designers cannot be indefinite and will have to be limited to the improvement of one or more services at a time.

A wise client would ensure that they have priority access to a skilled team for continuously maintaining and improving the new digital ecosystem. And that would represent an extension of the urban ecosystem with additional self-maintenance and self-improvement services.

Concurrent Design Mode

The ecosystem designers should be organised in three teams working concurrently on (1) requirements specifications, (2) the design and (3) the commissioning of improved services, timing the work as follows.

Whenever the design of the improvement of a service is completed, the requirements specification for the improvement of the next service is ready for design.

Whenever the commissioning of the improved service is completed, the design for the improvement of the next service is ready for commissioning.

Let's assume that the critical service selected for the improvement is the ambulance service.

Designing Ontology

The design begins with outlining ontology for the ambulance service, which involves:

Selecting *object classes* (ambulance vehicle, ambulance crew, crew member, ambulance equipment, route, road, hospital, patient, relative)

Identifying *relations* (crew belongs to vehicle, equipment belongs to crew, vehicle follows route)

Defining *properties* of object classes (for a crew member: id, qualifications, availability)

It is prudent at this stage to write *scripts* for agents, which should also be stored in ontology as properties of object classes, and ready for agents to pick them up when given a task to perform.

All policies, rules and regulations guiding the delivery of services should be also stored in ontology.

A Peek into the Design of a Digital Twin

To design the digital twin means to design the whole digital infrastructure that supports the exchange of meaningful messages among, potentially, hundreds of thousands of agents. The choice of technology is vital, and our recent switch to Python and Microservices brought considerable gains: the development time has been almost halved!

A digital twin is a place where digital agents negotiate among themselves how to allocate resources to demands. The process is rapid and, in principle, not repeatable. The conditions, under which negotiations between agents are conducted, often change during the negotiations. In this respect, a digital world is like Heraclitus' river: no digital agent can enter the same digital world twice.

In the digital world of an ambulance service, the matching of crew members to crews, crews to ambulance vehicles, ambulance vehicles to hospitals, roads to routes, patients to hospitals, etc. is done by exchange of messages between relevant agents.

To achieve adaptivity, the matching of demands to resources is done by communication between digital agents rather than by computation. If, for example, a road to the selected hospital is blocked by excessive traffic, the road agent of the blocked road will immediately let other road agents know of a problem and trigger a wave of renegotiations between affected agents to determine a new route to the hospital. If a new route is too long, agents may decide to negotiate a different hospital destination.

The key advantage of this type of rescheduling is that parts of the ambulance service ecosystem not affected by the road closure continue functioning as though no disruption occurred.

All scheduling decisions made in the digital twin by digital agents are sent to the real world, preferred method being messaging to smartphones or directly to relevant "things" (as in the Internet of Things).

What is described here is just a minute part of the design process, hopefully sufficient to demonstrate how complex adaptive technology offers a considerable advantage over conventional batch-mode optimisers.

Extending the Initial Design

Scheduling of ambulance vehicles is easily extended to cover, for example, the scheduling of hospital staff and facilities that are required by patients brought in by the ambulance vehicles. We just need an additional swarm of digital agents to do this job. And then, of course, we can add more swarms of digital agents to schedule other hospital resources such as operating theatres, etc. The design should advance step by step, each step proven in practice before the next one is commissioned.

Case Study 2: Real-Time Scheduler for Seagoing Tankers

The Problem

Our client was a management company operating one of the largest fleets of very large crude carrier (VLCC) oil tankers consisting of more than 40 ships and representing just below 10% of world seagoing tanker capacity.

The fleet was used to transport crude oil from Gulf to east and west coasts of the USA and from Columbia to Europe and Asia.

Scheduling of tankers was done by a team of five very experienced and skilled dispatchers. Planning and operations teams managing the fleet, as well as the fleet itself, were spread across many different locations and time zones.

The oil transportation market, in which our client operated, was subject to frequent and unpredictable fluctuations in transportation fees.

There were many other unpredictable factors affecting tanker operation, not least queues of vessels frequently forming in front of the entrance into the Panama Canal and fluctuation of fees for passing through the Canal related to the length of queues. Tankers belonging to our client were too big to enter the Canal loaded, and therefore, they had to unload a part of their cargo, which was then transferred to the other end of the Canal through a pipeline and re-loaded into the tanker.

Due to many interdependencies between different components of the schedule, small changes in one part of the schedule could have repercussions in other parts of the schedule, which were difficult to trace.

Resources were highly constrained: vessels had fixed parameters (capacity and types of cargo) that had to be considered when developing a schedule. Moreover, different customers and vessels had different preferences, which had to be taken into account. For example, some vessel owners had blacklists of ports into which their tankers were not allowed to enter, whilst some ports did not allow the loading or unloading of vessels, which were not fully insured.

Because of the high cost of scheduling mistakes, the requirement was for schedules to be easy to understand, justify, explain and modify by dispatchers.

The event that prompted the client to think seriously about purchasing a scheduler was a prospect of losing services of their key dispatcher due to sudden illness.

Optimal scheduling was perceived to be a computationally complex (NP-hard) problem, and, as a consequence, the use of conventional schedulers was not feasible.

The Solution

The global oil transportation market in which our client operated was highly complex. It was obvious that the client required an adaptive event-driven multi-agent scheduler, which we developed and commissioned. This was our first major application and the first ever real-time scheduler for seagoing vessels.

The scheduler consisted of a digital twin and a knowledge base. Digital twin was populated by the following agents:

Fleet agent (enterprise agent), which is primarily concerned with the prioritisation of orders and resources with a view to maximising enterprise value

Order agent, which searches for the most appropriate resources (vessels, crew) to meet the order, taking into account delivery deadline and cost of the resource (including idle runs, fuelling, etc.)

Route agent, which creates the optimal route for tankers considering deadlines, distances, fuelling locations and idle runs

Tanker agent, which ensures the best possible utilisation of the vessel

Competitor agent, which monitors the pricing of competing fleets and ensures that the client's pricing is competitive

Cargo agent, which ensures that the cargo is loaded into tankers with appropriate attributes considering cargo size, type of oil and transportation fees

Crew agent, which searches for the required crew for tankers considering routing, crew specification, cost per day and tanker schedule

Port agent, which ensures that only tankers that are cleared for entry into ports are scheduled to enter into it, considering mainly political and insurance issues

Fuelling agent, which searches for the best fuelling locations balancing fuel costs and cost of reaching the fuelling locations

All allocation decisions are made by negotiation between competent agents. For example, order agents, cargo agents and tanker agents negotiate the allocation of tankers to orders, whilst order agents, tanker agents, route agents, port agents and fuelling agents negotiate routes for each tanker.

If a tanker fails and needs repair, the tanker agent sends messages to all affected order agents informing them of the disruption. Order agents then renegotiate the allocation of vessels, routes, crew and other resources to meet order requirements.

If fuel price unexpectedly changes at the selected fuelling location, the fuelling agent sends messages to the affected tanker agents, which in turn renegotiate the routes to switch fuelling to a cheaper location.

Knowledge base consisted of ontology and a database. A fragment of ontology for scheduling of tankers is shown in Fig. 4.3. Classes of objects depicted are Tanker, Home Country, Client, Owner, Order, Route, Cargo, Port of Loading, Destination Port, Fuelling Location and Current State.

Before our scheduler was implemented, the client had in place a centralised database where all information relevant to scheduling was stored and regularly updated. This database was retained as the main repository of information and acted as a communication hub through which our scheduler received and sent scheduling messages to the rest of the business.

Each tanker has a terminal directly connected to the scheduling database. Locations of tankers are monitored by GPS and recorded in the scheduling database.

Dispatchers communicate with clients by phone and enter manually their orders and other relevant information into the scheduler database.

Client managers monitored fleet operation via screens connected to our scheduler.

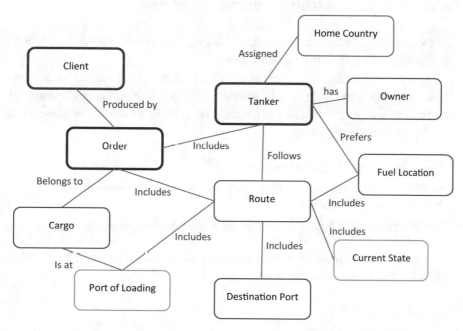

Fig. 4.3 A fragment of tanker ontology

Results

Our first industrial adaptive scheduler achieved commendable savings for the client: a reduction of 3 days of idle runs, per tanker, annually. Taking into account the cost of idle runs per tanker, per day, for 40 tankers, the savings generated a return on investment of less than 6 months.

There were other substantial savings more difficult to quantify. Our scheduler reduced significantly delays of oil deliveries and consequently payments of delay penalties.

Domain knowledge on running an oil transportation business was for the first time collected and organised in ontology in a computer-readable format and with editing facilities, which enabled easy updating by programmers.

The scheduler was designed to work in autonomous mode or in a decision support mode.

When in decision support mode, the requirement was that dispatchers should be provided with feasible scheduling options and cargo delivery price during a telephone conversation with a potential client. That was achieved. The scheduler typically requires few seconds to several minutes to complete the analysis and come up with costing of feasible scheduling options.

Case Study 3: AI-Based Epidemic Simulator

AI-based simulators are an essential tool for exploring options when developing a strategy, a tactical plan or a design.

Based on the notion that epidemic is a process of allocating victims to viruses and that viruses attack in groups, it is possible to design a complex adaptive simulator, say an *epidemic simulator*, capable of calculating infection rates for a variety of contexts:

- Open spaces (gardens, streets, beaches)
- Closed spaces (homes, theatres, cinemas, restaurants, pubs, hospitals, care homes, slaughterhouses)

In addition, the simulator would be capable of answering questions (taking into account the capability of viruses to mutate)—how much, and at what cost, infection rate would be reduced.

- By lockdown?
- By social distancing?

- By face masks?
- By testing?
- By other means?

Simulating wars between a group of viruses and a team of protection strategists would be an excellent way of learning how to manage an epidemic.

The architecture of an epidemic simulator is shown in Fig. 4.4.

The *simulated world* is a computer-readable dynamic description of the social context within which infection rate is calculated. For example, a group of restaurants is represented as a network with clusters. Each individual restaurant is represented as a cluster (in which infected and non-infected clients and employees interact). Connections between clusters represent flows of infected and non-infected clients and restaurant employees between restaurants.

The *digital world* is a digital twin of the simulated world in which a *digital agent* (a computational object) is assigned to each infected (infection agent) and each non-infected human being (victim agent) of the simulated world. The allocation of victim agents to infection agents (infection flow pattern) is calculated using domain knowledge stored in the knowledge base.

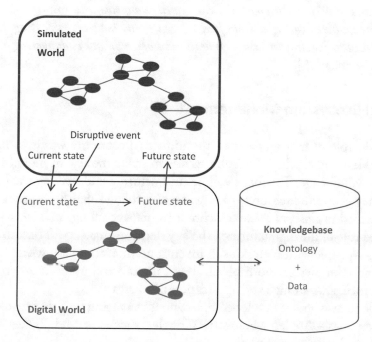

Fig. 4.4 Complex adaptive epidemic simulator

The *knowledge base* is the key element of the simulator, where all that is known about the coronavirus epidemic is collected and organised as epidemic ontology, which can be updated whenever needed, without interrupting simulation.

Digital Ecosystem Ownership

As intellectual capital replaces money as the key economic resource, it is very likely that the importance of knowledge workers who invest their expertise into day-to-day running of a digital ecosystem (knowledge stakeholders) will increase on the expense of shareholders who invest only their money (investment stakeholders). It is also likely that the local community will be involved in the business ownership via community representatives (community stakeholders).

Digital Ecosystem Mission

Since the new generation of knowledge workers is much more socially and environmentally aware, it is expected that the key mission of smart digital ecosystems will be to *support the connected, adaptive and sustainable society, which is capable of cost-effectively feeding, watering, housing, educating, keeping in good health, moving and employing its members without endangering our natural environment* [5].

Digital Ecosystem Management

The main role of management in the industrial economy was/is to increase shareholders value, which basically means to make money. In digital society, the role will change. The focus will be on nurturing and making the best use of the key economic resource—knowledge. It follows that professional managers trained in classical business schools to manage money making will have a limited role in the digital future. The key decision-makers will be knowledge workers—people with high skills in invention; innovation; knowledge extraction from data; design, both physical and digital; and other knowledge creation, processing, storage and application processes.

Just look at who has developed and who is managing leading flagship digital companies—Apple, Microsoft, Google, Facebook and Tesla—mainly exceptional knowledge workers.

One of the pioneers of digital revolution, Marc Andreessen, who at the University of Illinois developed NCSA Mosaic, one of the first graphic web browsers, and who in Silicon Valley launched Netscape, a predecessor to Google, recently gave an interview to McKinsey & Company in which he advised "Find the smartest technologists in the company and make them CEO".

Key Points

1. Natural ecosystems are complex—they self-organise to adapt to changes in their environment, to resist attacks and to coevolve with other systems, often for million years.
2. AI enables us to transform organisations into smart digital ecosystems which behave similarly to natural ecosystems and are fit to operate in complex environments.

References

1. Ellis, Erle C. "Ecology in an Anthropogenic Biosphere." Ecological Monographs 2015. 85 (3): 287–331. https://doi.org/10.1890/14-2274.1.
2. Rzevski, G., P. Skobelev, "Managing Complexity". WIT Press, Southampton, Boston, 2014. ISBN 978-1-84564-936-4.
3. Moore, JF, "Predators and Prey: a new Ecology of Competition". Harvard Business Review, 1993.
4. Rzevski, G, Skobelev, P, Batishchev, S, Orlov, A.: "A Framework for Multi-Agent Modelling of Virtual Organisations". In Camarinha-Matos, L M and Afsarmanesh, H (eds), Processes and foundations for Virtual Organisations, Kluwer Academic Publishers, 2003, ISBN 978-1-4020-7638-1, pp. 253-260.
5. Rzevski, G., "Intelligent Multi-Agent Platform for Designing Digital Ecosystems". In Vladimir Marik, Petr Kadera, George Rzevski, Alois Zolti, Gabriele Anderst-Kotsis, A Min Yjoa, Ismail Khalil (eds), Proceedings of the 9th International Conference, HoloMAS 2019, Linz, Austria, August 26 – 29, 2019, pp. 29-41. LNAI 11710.
6. Glaschenko, A., Ivaschenko, A., Rzevski, G., Skobelev, P. "Multi-Agent Real Time Scheduling System for Taxi Companies". *Proc. of 8th Int. Conf on Autonomous Agents and Multiagent Systems (AAMAS 2009)*, Decker, Sichman, Sierra, and Castelfranchi (eds.), May 10–15, 2009, Budapest, Hungary. ISBN: 978-0-9817381-6-1, pp. 29-35.

7. Rzevski, G., Soloviev, V., Skobelev, P. & Lakhin, O., "Complex adaptive logistics for the international space station", International Journal of Design & Nature and Ecodynamics, Volume 11 No. 3 (2016), pp. 459-472. ISSN: 1755-7437.

8. Minakov, I., Rzevski, G., Skobelev, P., Volman, S., "Creating Contract Templates for Car Insurance Using Multi-Agent Based Text Understanding and Clustering". *Lecture Notes in Computer Science, Volume 4659, Holonic and Multi-Agent Systems for Manufacturing. Third International Conference on Industrial Applications of Holonic and Multi-Agent Systems, HoloMAS 2007*, Regensburg, Germany, September 2007, Springer, ISBN 978-3-540-74478-8, pp. 361-371.

9. Hettige, B., Karunananda, A. S., Rzevski, G. "Multi Agent Framework for Development of Machine Translation Systems". 2013, 8th International Conference on Science & Education ICCSE 2013. Colombo, Sri Lanka.

10. Madsen, B., Skobelev, P., Rzevski, G., and Tsarev, A. "Real-Time Multi-agent Forecasting and Replenishment Solution for LEGOs Branded Retail Outlets." *International Journal of Software Innovation*, Volume 1 Issue 2, ISSN: 2166-7100, pp. 28-39. IGI Global, 2013.

11. Andreev, S., Rzevski, G., Shveykin, P., Skobelev, P., Yankov, I. "Multi-Agent Scheduler for Rent-A-Car Companies". Lecture Notes in Computer Science, volume 5696, Holonic and Multi-Agent Systems for Manufacturing: Forth International Conference on Industrial Applications of Holonic and Multi-Agent Systems, HoloMAS 2009, Linz, Austria. Springer, ISBN 978-3-540-74478-8, pp. 305-314.

12. V. Shpilevoy, A. Shishov, P. Skobelev, E. Kolbova, D. Kazanskaia, Y. Shepilov, A. Tsarev. Multi-agent system "Smart Factory" for real-time workshop management in aircraft jet engines production // Proceedings of the 11th IFAC Workshop on Intelligent Manufacturing Systems (IMS'13), May 22-24, 2013, São Paulo, Brazil, 2013.

13. Rzevski, G., P. Skobelev, "Intelligent Adaptive Schedulers for Railways", International Journal of Transport Development and Integration, Volume 1 No 3, (2017), pp. 414-420. ISSN: 2058-8305.

5

We Are in Transition from Industrial to Digital Economy

Introduction

Every major stepwise transition in the socioeconomic evolution is difficult, and the transition from the industrial to digital economy is not different.

Globalisation, the legacy of the industrial economy, has increased *physical connectivity* between suppliers and customers from different, remote countries and created long intercontinental supply chains using huge container ships, cargo flights and juggernaut lorries. And it intensified business travel.

Building large-scale factories in developing countries to reduce manufacturing costs created unintended consequences:

Waste of energy and increased pollution to a level that is unsustainable.

Amplified butterfly effect—the notorious example being the rapid spread of coronavirus infection, which converted a single case in Wuhan into a global pandemic in a matter of days.

Vulnerability of nations in a crisis—the coronavirus pandemic and the war in Ukraine showed that, in a global crisis, nations focus on what they think is the best for them, ignoring needs of others. Even within the European Union, there were cases where nations competed rather than cooperated for access to resources in short supply, such as protective equipment for Covid. Locating our factories in faraway places made us truly vulnerable during conflicts. The war in Ukraine demonstrated that globalisation, as practised, is too dangerous. Some nations exposed themselves by relying heavily for their energy supply on a single country.

© The Author(s), under exclusive license to Springer Nature Switzerland AG 2023
G. Rzevski, *The Future is Digital*, https://doi.org/10.1007/978-3-031-37810-2_5

On top of globalisation, digital communication technology—the Internet and mobile phones—*increased the digital connectivity* of the world population. At the time of writing this chapter, there were nearly 5 billion Internet users, which was over 60% of the total world population of just under 8 billion.

The combination of the two—the physical and digital connectivity—caused an exponential increase in complexity of the socioeconomic environment in which we live and work.

Exactly as Stephen Hawking, the holder of Newton's chair in physics at Cambridge University, warned us, "the 21st century will be the century of complexity".

Complexity Creates Uncertainty and Unpredictability; We Long for Stability and a Clear Cause-Effect Relationship

The negative consequences of the increased complexity hit the unprepared population used to relatively stable economic cycles of the industrial era. It is not surprising therefore that voters reacted by blaming politicians without realising that the tide of socioeconomic evolution is not under their control.

Nevertheless, mistakes have been made by politicians who were simply not equipped to handle the increased complexity of the world. Here are few examples:

Setting targets for the transfer from petrol and diesel to the electric propulsion of all vehicles without investing into the expansion of electricity supply networks

Setting targets for net zero without securing safe energy supply for the transition period

Allowing to be critically dependent on energy supply or the production of consumer and infrastructure goods from a single source

The problem was made worst by the traditionally trained experts—economists, political scientists, lawyers and epidemiologists—who viewed the world through the industrial era lenses and appeared to be unaware that the planet has turned into a complex, volatile structure in which a change in any connection between constituent elements may be amplified and propagate in any direction and rapidly produce unpredictable global effects.

High complexity of the current geopolitical system and the Internet-based global market have substantially contributed to extreme events such as:

Global financial crisis of 2008
Rapidly spreading pandemic of 2020
Economic impact of Ukraine war of 2022
A surge in mass migration

Let's look briefly at each through the lenses of complexity science.

Financial Crisis of 2008

As described in chapter on complexity, the financial crisis of 2008 was caused by a *drift into failure* of financial services. To gain bonuses, some loans appear to have been offered to clients who could not repay them—*toxic loans*. Debts gradually reached the tipping point and turned into an unstoppable global crisis [1].

Many books were written about the crisis providing explanations from a variety of viewpoints none showing any understanding how complexity of the global financial system masked the build-up to the crisis.

Only a rudimentary knowledge of complexity science is required to grasp how easy it is to prevent the next financial crisis. And yet, the resistance to new ideas that contradict the well-established mindset of experts in financial services may make the new crisis even worse than the last one.

Technology for preventing a global financial crisis has been developed based on *emergent AI*. These systems are capable of checking loan applicants' financial circumstances and approving loans [2].

AI doesn't cheat to get a bonus (unless designed to do so). And it is cheaper to employ than human resources.

Covid Pandemic of 2020

A rapidly spreading pandemic is a typical result of a butterfly effect—a single small disruption at one end of the planet causes massive infection all over the world in a matter of days. We were not prepared when the recent Covid pandemic occurred.

Are we prepared to face the next?

My view is that current models of coronavirus pandemic are inadequate because modellers have attempted to model a complex process—epidemic—ignoring principles of complexity science.

Shortcomings of current coronavirus epidemic mathematical models, as perceived by the author, are:

Different models provide radically different values for the average reproduction number R (infection rate).
Reproduction numbers for different social contexts are not calculated.
Virus adaptation and mutation are not covered.
Group behaviour of viruses and potential victims is ignored.
The cost-effectiveness of various protection policies is not investigated.

A good example, highly relevant to the modelling of virus behaviour, is a group of viruses deciding if they should stay longer in the cells of a victim or switch to a new host [3].

Here is how the article "The Secret Social Lives of Viruses", published on the website of the prestigious journal, *Nature*, on the 18th of June 2019, depicts a group of viruses making decisions: "the viruses …. were chattering away, passing notes to each other in a molecular language only they could understand. They were deciding together when to lie low in the host cell and when to replicate and burst out, in search of new victims".

Modellers ignored the fact that viruses attack in groups and that epidemic is an adaptive system—viruses when threatened (say, by lockdowns) adapt by mutating into a new version of itself, usually much more infectious.

A pandemic simulator that considers pandemic as a complex system, as described in Chap. 4 or similar, is an essential tool for the preparation for the next pandemic.

Invasion of Ukraine of 2022

The war in Ukraine is an extreme event hitting the complex global village.

Both sides in the conflict are major suppliers of agricultural products, and one side is a major supplier of energy (oil and gas). It is, therefore, inevitable that the war will have a major impact on the world trade at a critical point in time, just when the planet is slowly recovering from consequences of the major crisis, Covid.

No previous local invasion of a neighbour ever caused worldwide political disruptions of the kind, but then, the world was never so complex.

Figure 5.1 illustrates the high connectivity among world regions at the time when the war began. Globalisation increased the economic interdependency

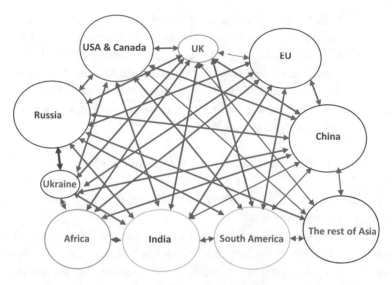

Fig. 5.1 Complexity of the geopolitical constellation at the time of invasion

of world regions and in the process, unwittingly, destroyed the self-sufficiency of nations, which is priceless during global crises such as a pandemic or a war.

Due to the complexity of the world, the invasion of Ukraine caused military and economic consequences on a large scale, most of them unintended. Military and political decision-makers ignored the high complexity of the geopolitical and economic constellation at the time, which is perhaps not surprising considering that during the last major conflict, the Cold War, the world was in a stable, rather than complex, situation as illustrated in Fig. 5.2.

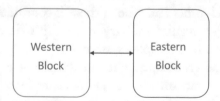

Fig. 5.2 Simple and stable geopolitical system during the Cold War

Is It Rational to Attempt to Recover Lost Territories by a Military Intervention?

Let's assume that the UK decides to invade France now to recover its lost territories—Normandy, Anjou and Bordeaux—which the UK legitimately acquired when Eleanor of Aquitaine married the Duke of Normandy who ascended to English throne as Henry the Second Plantagenet in 1154.

The idea is of course absurd; nevertheless, even more absurdly, let us assume that you, the reader, are asked to plan the invasion. Would it occur to you to check history books to learn how other invaders fared recently?

It did occur to me. And I have found that *since Napoleonic times, no nation that started a war managed to win it.*

Napoleon lost in Spain and Russia in a guerrilla warfare and was finished at Waterloo.

Franz Joseph not only lost the First World War, but his Austro-Hungarian Empire was dismembered.

Hitler was reduced to killing his dog, his mistress and himself in an underground bunker when he lost the Second World War. At Stalingrad, his army of millions could not subdue Russian guerrilla-like resistance.

Japan surrendered after two atomic bomb hits.

The Soviet Union ran out of Afghanistan after 9 years of guerrilla warfare.

The USA lost in Vietnam, again in a guerrilla warfare.

The UK and France could not regain the ownership of the Suez Canal in 1956.

Mighty NATO could not overpower guerrilla resistance in Iraq and Afghanistan.

After all these years, Israel still cannot win a guerrilla war with Palestine.

It is a pattern, isn't it?

Guerrilla is a Spanish word for a "small war", invented to describe how Spaniards fought Napoleon, by autonomous small groups and individuals cooperating with each other and who, although coordinated, were not under a central control, like regular military units. This description of guerrilla matches the definition of a complex system.

Remember? A system is complex if it consists of a diverse set of participants engaged in intense interaction without being centrally controlled.

Guerrilla warfare is therefore a complex system—and its complexity is a reason for its success.

Guerrilla resistance is adaptive and resilient. If you destroy one guerrilla unit, new units will spring into existence. Fighters unexpectedly attack the invaders where they are most vulnerable and disappear into thin air. They are protected by their own civilians.

Following the trend of unsuccessful invasions, the war in Ukraine brought no joy to the invader.

Declared objectives, to rapidly invade Ukraine and depose its government, could not be achieved, and at the time of writing this text, the invasion stalled, and defenders managed to recover a considerable part of the lost territory.

Within 6 months, it is estimated that Russia has lost more soldiers than the Soviet Union during the 9-year war in Afghanistan (15,000 dead; 35,000 wounded then). How many more young people will lose their lives or be maimed until the end of the war? For what?

Millions of immigrants overwhelmed neighbouring countries. How many will return?

The invasion caused destruction of valuable assets on a vast scale. Reconstruction will require enormous financial resources. Who is going to pay?

Western democracies closed ranks and agreed on almost total boycott of Russian business, culture and sport. How long will it take for Russia to be accepted by the West as a partner again?

Russian citizens and businesses are left without access to Western technology, finances, knowledge and goods (including spare parts for Airbus aircraft on which all Russian airlines depend).

NATO emerged much stronger and, in particular, its East wing.

Economic consequences of the war are felt worldwide.

The population of Western democracies, which were dangerously dependent on Russian energy supply, have suffered a sharp increase in costs of gas. This coincided with the increase of inflation due, in part, to the generous government handouts to compensate loss of earnings during Covid lockdowns.

Interruptions of the international food supply chains fuelled food shortages and price increases.

Supply of essential agricultural products, such as grain to African and Asian countries, was temporary interrupted.

And military considerations?

The conflict confirmed that attacking armies are never as strongly motivated as those that defend their homes.

It soon became obvious that the modern warfare is too complex to be under the centralised command. Delegation of operational decision-making to commanders close to action is much more effective.

The war gradually became a testing ground for new weapons, mostly those supplied to Ukraine by the West.

Mass Migration

In the twenty-first century, we have built a complex, connected world in which individuals, communities and movements, *such as mass migration*, have access to advanced communication technologies (data streaming, smartphones, emails, the Internet, search engines and social websites) and thus can exchange news and gossip and conduct business among themselves with (almost) the speed of light.

The mass migration is clearly a complex system. Observing migration through the lenses of complexity science helps to determine its properties and to discover which, if any, intervention could lead to a desirable outcome.

Mass migration from Asia and Africa to Europe is likely to accelerate and therefore represents a threat to socioeconomic stability.

Niall Ferguson (*Sunday Times*, 6 January 2019) cites a Gallup survey in 2017, according to which more than 700 million adults around the world would like to move permanently to another country. 23% would prefer to move to a European country and 21% to the USA.

It is not surprising that in some target countries, there is a strong opposition to the increase in the flow of immigrants. Recent polling by the Pew Research Center shows that only 16% of the UK population would welcome more immigrants.

In the same article, Ferguson writes "if the choice is between open borders and defensive walls, history suggests walls—and those who build them—will win".

This statement can be considered as sensible only if we give it a charitable interpretation that "defensive wall" is a metaphor covering all interventions, which could prevent undesirable visitors crossing open borders, rather than literally building physical walls.

Let's first establish that mass migration is indeed a complex system.

As stated earlier, a complex system (or a complex group) is open (interacts with its environment); consists of a large number of diverse components, called agents, which are richly connected with each other and engaged in intensive interaction; has no central control; and behaves unpredictably, but not random—it follows recognisable patterns.

Mass migration has all the characteristics of a complex system listed above.

It is open—it feeds on information on where it is best to migrate and on the availability of clandestine support for illegal entry into target countries, including hiring of transport.

It consists of a wide variety of constituent migrants connected using latest communication technology and engaged in continuous interaction—sharing latest news, gossip and opportunities.

It has organisers, leaders, but *no central control.*

It behaves opportunistically, adapting to everchanging, hostile environment, and its overall behaviour is therefore unpredictable but not random.

Complex systems are, of course, highly adaptive, and when efforts were intensified to prevent migrants to be smuggled from France to the UK in lorries, they rapidly discovered a new route across the Channel—using stolen French fishing boats and small inflatable vessels.

Current migration from Asia and Africa to Europe appears to be triggered and driven by many related factors. Here are some:

Local military conflicts often caused or made worse by military interventions by big Western and/or Eastern powers (the Russian invasion of Ukraine, within first few days, created estimated several million migrants).

Very low living standards.

Very high unemployment.

Sense of adventure and curiosity, the very same that drove early British explorers to discover wonders of the world and early British Empire builders to conquer new territories.

Information reaching potential migrants that in Europe living standards are much higher (potential migrants have access to modern communication technology).

Information that the UK offers the best chance to find employment; British employment laws and regulations are very liberal, which is one of the reasons why migrants try to get across the Channel by all possible and impossible means.

Availability of a clandestine network of resources supporting practical aspects of mass migration such as transport and support for illegal entry into target countries.

All factors identified here are long term. Local military conflicts, low living standards and high unemployment are likely to persist, unless concerted efforts are made to help.

Illegal networks of smugglers will make sure that flow of migrants does not dry up.

Do we need immigrants?

Let's consider the UK. Other countries may have similar or other needs.

In the UK, yes, we do.

The UK economy is in transition from industrial to knowledge-based service economy; knowledge services skills and, in particular, digital technology skills will be increasingly in demand, and this demand is easy to meet by immigrants with appropriate profiles.

The UK healthcare industry needs additional doctors, nurses and supporting staff.

The UK economy requires a steady supply of workers with *simple manual skills* for agriculture, catering and hospitality industries (farm workers, waiters, cleaners) and for support of households (domestic help, gardeners, plumbers, electricians).

According to many rankings, British universities are among the very best in the world, and they attract international talent; talented staff and students are required to maintain high-quality teaching and research, and diversity promotes tolerance of foreign cultures among British students and encourages acceptance of British values by foreign youth.

But we have to be careful.

Additional resources are required for selecting and then absorbing large numbers of immigrants.

We must learn how to help immigrants to integrate into host culture and avoid resentment towards immigrants in the country.

All the above considerations must take into account that within the next 10 years, artificial intelligence is likely to take over about 40% of current full-time jobs and create many more new jobs for which we shall need new skills and we know very little if anything about these new skills.

In the context of how to select immigrants, one should not forget that productivity, as calculated under industrial conditions, is not a good criterion since the UK is, primarily, a service-providing economy.

In service industries, a larger number of workers per customer are often required to provide excellence.

Here are two examples:

Elite universities have a high staff-to-student ratio (low productivity of staff members per student), an essential feature for providing high-quality education.

In a restaurant aspiring to provide high-quality experience, one needs guest receptionists, food servers, sommeliers, chefs, sous-chefs, dessert chefs, etc., in other words, high staff-to-customer ratio (low productivity of staff members per customer).

Mass migration creates a number of issues.

Integration

One of the key problems with immigration is the conflict between cultures—the host country culture and the immigrant's culture. Using parlance of complexity science, *culture limits freedom of behaviour of its members*; it imposes norms on how people dress, marry, worship and eat and therefore emphasises differences between the hosts and the immigrants.

In all complex groups, there is a propensity for members with similar features to cluster. The UK immigrants are not exceptions. For example, in London, we have prominent immigrant clusters—the Polish in Ealing, the Indian in Southall, the French in South Kensington and so on. Clusters of foreign culture, once formed, is almost impossible to disperse. They prevent, or slow down, the integration of immigrants into the host culture.

Resources Required to Absorb Immigrants

The increase in population caused by immigration requires proportional increase in resources for housing, feeding, watering, heating, cooling, dressing, refuse removal, education, healthcare, transport and entertainment, which, of course, reduces green areas (fields and forests), increases pollution, consumes energy, generates CO_2 and endangers water supply, which may or may not be compensated by the potential increase in wealth creation.

Resources Required for Receiving and Processing Immigrants

Since it is very likely that the number of potential immigrants who will attempt to reach their target country illegally, by hiding in containers, by crossing the Channel in a variety of boats or by any other way, will considerably increase, there will be a need to organise very large immigrant reception and processing facilities as well as the return transport for those rejected.

We Need a Strategy to Control Mass Migration

Mass migration is too complex to be regulated by ad hoc unilateral actions.

To control the flow of immigrants, it will be necessary to devise a comprehensive immigration strategy.

Determine the number of immigrants with skills required by the economy, taking into account the fact that Western economies are undergoing a major transition from trading in mass-produced goods (industrial economy) to transacting in knowledge-based services (information economy).

Find financial resources and build required infrastructure needed for receiving, processing, transporting back those who are rejected and absorbing those who are accepted.

Plan how to initiate and manage interventions aimed at controlling the flow of migrants, as identified below.

If factors that trigger and drive the flow of immigrants from Asia and Africa to the West have been identified correctly, we can reduce the propensity to migrate in the long run by the following.

Stopping all military interventions, which are fundamentally cruel and useless; remember that no nation that recently started a war won it.

Investing into the infrastructure and businesses in regions that represent major sources of migration with a view to improving living standards and increasing employment opportunities; an additional benefit would be the creation of new markets.

Acting to prevent the operation of clandestine migration support networks employing methods similar to those used in antiterrorist defence.

The immigration strategy will have to coevolve with the global geopolitical and economic environment.

How to Survive and Prosper During the Transition

As remarked earlier, the unstoppable and irreversible social evolution follows a pattern. The pattern is hidden in an apparently chaotic behaviour of our socioeconomic environment, but, nevertheless, it is there and can be recognised by an informed eye. It tells us that *the future is digital.*

It follows that if we want the economic growth, we must urgently develop a digital strategy based on the following three elements.

Creating economic growth by focusing on digital services and AI
Gradually withdrawing from globalisation and maximising national self-sufficiency
Ensuring that the prosperity created by digital industry is shared among all

Creating Economic Growth by Focusing on Digital Services and AI

Why Digital Services and AI?

Whilst the world is in the early stage of digital transformation, the demand for digital services and AI outstrips supply by a very large margin. Rich opportunities for the early adopters.

Finding skilled knowledge workers should not be too difficult. Digital industry is unique in offering opportunities for participants to work *from office, from home* or as *digital nomads*. An estimated 30 million of digital workers currently work full time online and, at the same time, move across the planet from one country to another making use of easy-to-obtain *digital visas*.

Hiring digital workers is not conditional on the availability of local talents.

But, of course, instead of being a nomad, the knowledge worker can stay put, enjoy the local culture and, if there is no local opportunity, *work for a faraway digital employer.*

It follows that every local community needs a digital growth centre to spot and nurture digital talents—finding for them a willing employer is not a problem. Training the youth in digital skills and helping them to find a *local or remote employment* is the fastest way of levelling up.

The advantage of being an early adopter is best illustrated by the economic success of California.

Californian GDP

Let's follow the example of the federal state of California. At the time of writing this book, the USA, as a whole, was not in a perfect economic shape and was deeply troubled by political conflicts. At the same time, the GDP of California surpassed the GDP of France and the UK and was just about to exceed the GDP of Germany.

How could the economy of a federal state with less than 40 million inhabitants create consistently more wealth per annum than the economies of European nations with 60–80 million citizens?

The answer is simple: *by focusing on digital technology and, particularly, on AI.*

The diagram below illustrates the rapid growth of the GDP of California compared to the UK (data sources are World Bank website and Wikipedia) (Fig. 5.3).

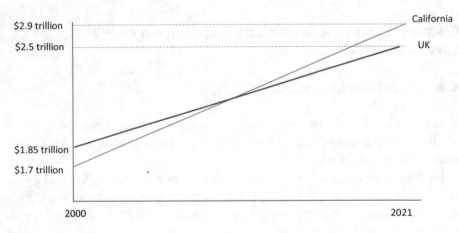

Fig. 5.3   Comparing the GDP growth of California and the UK

Reducing Participation in Globalisation and Maximising National Self-Sufficiency

Cutting our nonessential physical connectivity to the rest of the world by bringing the manufacture of critically important goods home and by developing local energy sources would *reduce economic dependence on other nations*. As a bonus, it will reduce the transport of goods across the planet and thus decrease global energy wastage and pollution.

International trade should be maintained by predominantly transacting in knowledge-based services rather than in goods (more on this topic in Chap. 6).

Ensuring That the Prosperity Created by Digital Industry Is Shared Among All

There is no doubt that knowledge workers will benefit from the economic success of digital transformation. The problem is that others may not. There is a need to support those that cannot or do not want to be retrained.

We should again learn from California, but this time from their mistakes. They seem to have failed to protect the weak, and the contrast between rich and deprived neighbourhoods is unbelievable.

In a prosperous and civilised society, there should be no poverty.

Artificial intelligence can help in creating a prosperous society, but we have to apply natural intelligence to find a new way of eliminating poverty without high taxes that kill entrepreneurship.

Nations Cannot Be Forced to Go Digital But Should Not Be Prevented

Pressurising a nation to accept a new technology is counterproductive. On the other hand, preventing, or unduly restricting, individual entrepreneurs who have energy and enthusiasm for the new technology is plainly wrong.

The outcry against AI caused by the release of chatbots should not result in restricting the use of AI. It should bring about legislation *punishing those who misuse the new tool.*

Key Points

1. Globalisation and widespread use of digital communication technology have caused a rapid increase in complexity of the geopolitical, socioeconomic and military environment in which we live and work. As a result, we suffer from frequent unpredictable disruptive events and occasional extreme events, such as the global financial crisis of 2008, Covid of 2020 and war in Europe of 2021.
2. To prosper, we need to focus on developing a strong digital business sector that brings benefits to everyone in a country.

References

1. Rzevski, G., "Using Tools of Complexity Science to Diagnose the Current Financial Crisis". Optoelectronics, Instrumentation and Data Processing, Vol.46 (2010), No. 2. ISSN 8756-6990.
2. Rzevski, G.; Skobelev, P.; Zhilyaev, A. "Emergent Intelligence in Smart Ecosystems: Conflicts Resolution by Reaching Consensus in Resource Management". Mathematics 2022, 10, 1923. https://doi.org/10.3390/math10111923.
3. Dolgin E., "The Secret Social Lives of Viruses". Nature 570, 290–292 (2019).

6

The New Digital Economy

Introduction

In the industrial society, to achieve economies of scale, the natural propensity to live and work in small groups was ignored. Whenever possible, people were packed into large units—large factories, large corporations, large schools and universities—much too large for the liking of many, who felt frustrated being seen as cogs in a machine, rather than as distinct individuals, as perceptively described by Schumacher in his seminal book *Small is Beautiful* [1].

The legacy of the industrial society is far too many large and rigid corporations, institutions and administrations, which can only operate effectively in low-complexity markets, where the demand and supply are stable and therefore predictable, and the operation can be planned well in advance, often using standard enterprise resource planning (ERP) systems, which are sold off the shelf.

Organisations designed for the *mass production* of a limited range of products and *mass administration* are *too slow* to respond positively to frequent disruptions, which are an integral part of complexity.

This is a serious issue.

However, by creating issues, complexity opens up new opportunities.

Every complexity issue is, in fact, an opportunity to find the best way of resolving the issue.

A serious issue is a serious opportunity.

It is a huge economic opportunity to transform rigid, top-down controlled corporations and administrations into adaptive networks of organisational units capable of performing successfully in a complex world [2].

© The Author(s), under exclusive license to Springer Nature Switzerland AG 2023
G. Rzevski, *The Future is Digital*, https://doi.org/10.1007/978-3-031-37810-2_6

Such a large-scale transformation is bound to create many satellite employment opportunities—researching, advising, training, supporting, financing, marketing, evaluating the process and, of course, developing the essential digital tools.

A real economic Aladdin's cave.

Trading in Knowledge Will Be the Main Global Economic Activity

Digital technology enables packaging knowledge into *digital formats*, such as the World Wide Web, pdf, electronic books, podcasts, posts, videos, webinars, tweets, Instagram messages, online lectures or software.

Digital coding enables *the cost-effective capture, storage, access and rapid distribution of knowledge* on an unprecedented scale. It creates a new opportunity for trading in intellectual services and thus originates a *knowledge economy*.

It is expected that this opportunity will be fully exploited and that intercontinental trading in goods will be gradually reduced and trading in knowledge increased.

Globalisation Will Be Replaced by a Global Economic Ecosystem

Globalisation, as currently practised, will be probably changed; its unintended consequences are too negative.

The world cannot afford to waste energy and generate pollution by unnecessary moving goods up and down the planet.

Rapid transmission of instabilities across continents and the amplification of disruptions are pausing dangers to all participants during global crises (pandemics, wars).

No nation should risk being excessively dependent on others for the supply of critical goods and energy.

To avoid issues created by globalisation, in addition to switching from trading in goods to trading in knowledge, it will be necessary to reconfigure the global trading network into a clustered network as shown in Fig. 6.1.

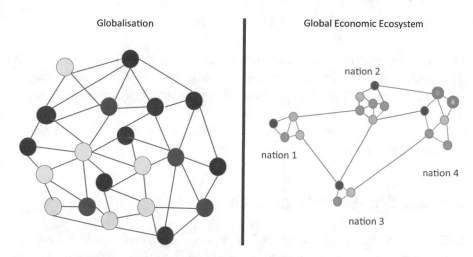

Fig. 6.1 Global economic ecosystem versus globalisation

Global economic ecosystem, illustrated by the diagram on the right, is an adaptive, resilient and sustainable global network of participating sovereign nations that compete or cooperate with each other depending on everchanging circumstances. If properly configured, it will behave like a natural ecosystem.

It is the system that can accommodate both friendly and unfriendly nations and even nations in a military conflict with each other. Just like a natural ecosystem, in which both lambs and wolves coexist.

My firm belief is that the pattern of failed invasions, described in Chap. 5, will, in time, turn nations against the war and ensure the peaceful world.

The global ecosystem satisfies the human propensity to live in cultural clusters—nations—and it is a far better arrangement for international trading than current globalisation, which directly connects producers and consumers across the world, bypassing nations. Temporarily cutting trade links between countries, in cases of conflicts, is less disruptive than severing direct connections between suppliers and customers.

The process of transformation of globalisation into global ecosystem is an evolutionary process that has already begun, as evidenced by post-pandemic efforts to make countries self-sufficient in critical healthcare products.

Digital Ecosystems of the Future

Digital transformation of traditional organisations has already sufficiently advanced, at least in some countries. It seems inevitable that in the digital economy, most participants will be organised as smart digital ecosystems, as described in Chap. 4.

Let's look at digital ecosystems that are likely to be the main contributors to the digital economy.

Knowledge-Based Services

Selling knowledge is usually referred to as providing knowledge-based service.

Here are some examples of knowledge-based services: software services, online search services, online socialising and dating services, online diagnosing and update services, online trading services, video conferencing services, broadband services, mobile communication services, research and development services, design services, extracting knowledge from data services, advising and consulting services, education and training services, financial services, project management services, marketing and PR services, event planning services, healthcare and social services, online legal services, online insurance services, online banking services, cyber security services, online travel services, online real estate services, publishing services, printing services and streaming and news providing services, to mention just a few.

Knowledge-based services will be also delivered face to face, for example, by lecturers, management consultants and decision support staff. Direct contacts between providers and recipients of knowledge are always highly beneficial. Online delivery, however, multiplies productivity of the service. A hybrid delivery will be preferred whenever possible.

Due to the digitising of all, or almost all, monitoring, detection, communication and decision-making functions within new products, such as electric cars, the value of the digital content of the product is likely to exceed the value of mechanical components. Therefore, the mechanical component of the product can be considered (from the valuation point of view), as just the *packaging of knowledge.*

Knowledge packaged in physical objects requires physical transport only once, to be delivered to a customer; the updates, performance tuning, diagnosis of faults and a good deal of maintenance can then be done online—a benefit for car owners and a substantial saving of energy.

I have singled out below knowledge-based services which will be of particular importance.

Educational Services

Let's repeat once more that in the digital economy, the key resource for success is knowledge [3]. This makes education the critically important activity.

The aim of education should be, perhaps, adjusted to emphasise the new role of knowledge. Students should be helped:

To perceive knowledge as intellectual capital, the essential resource for productive life and work
To understand the complex world in which they live and work
To develop their own value systems, creativity, attitude, independent thinking and communication and debating skills
To acquire work and life-oriented competences, appropriate for the contemporary complex world

What educational resources are required to achieve this aim?
We need:

Teachers who inspire and advise rather than instruct
Access to online masterclasses given by intellectual giants of the past and present for student to listen to and discuss
Access to intellectual treasures stored on the Internet, as sources of inspirations
Help from AI-based take-me-anywhere teaching and testing assistants

Decision Support Services

The main purpose of an administration is to *support decision-makers* in politics, business, healthcare, education, military, etc.

Current administrations are organised as specialised divisions and departments and managed by rigid hierarchies. Whilst that may have been a good idea under stable demand conditions, it is counterproductive in the current fast-changing world in which issues are complex and require rapid reaction and cross-departmental skills.

A new organisation is required to provide cost-effective decision support when dealing with unpredictable extreme events such as financial crises,

82   G. Rzevski

pandemics, mass vaccination, immigration, wars, cyberattacks, terrorism, temporary shortages and inflation.

The most effective way of organising administrators under new conditions is, perhaps, by transforming rigidly structured administration into a network of flexible, issue-oriented decision support units continuously adapting to everchanging demand.

Departments would assume a role of agents, responsible for looking after administrator's wellbeing and placing administrators with particular skills into appropriate issue-based units.

Decision support specialists themselves require support, which should be provided whenever possible by AI because it is reliable, rapid and cost-effective.

Examples include:

AI-based allocation of physical, human and financial resources to projects
AI-based production of document and handling of correspondence
AI-based project management systems
AI-based analytics for supporting administrative decisions
AI-based simulators for evaluating options when resolving an important issue
Decision support knowledge bases

Healthcare Services

AI can have the greatest impact in healthcare by drastically improving productivity in non-medical business processes, reducing non-medical workforce and supporting medical staff in areas such as diagnostics.

Opportunities are everywhere.

AI-based allocation of medical staff, medical equipment and medical materials to patients
AI-based scheduling of non-medical activities (purchasing, supplying, cleaning, maintenance)
AI-based production of document and handling of correspondence
AI-based project management systems
AI-based medical diagnostics
AI-based analytics for supporting healthcare decisions
AI-based simulators for evaluating options when planning changes or expansion of healthcare
Healthcare knowledge bases

It is well known that the current healthcare services are too expensive and that it is essential to improve the utilisation of high-value medical personnel and resources to enable its widespread use.

And in the UK, it is very important to reduce waiting for the appointment in the free at-point-of-use National Health Service.

My research shows that the largest cost reduction can be achieved by the AI-based real-time allocation of resources to everchanging demands. Intelligent real-time schedulers reduce waste by rapidly rescheduling affected resources (doctors, nurses, operating theatres, beds, specialist equipment, ambulances) whenever a cancellation, a change in demand or a resource failure occurs.

A good example of how AI can help with saving healthcare costs is an adaptive ambulance service—if a call is cancelled after an ambulance has already left the hospital to respond to that call, an adaptive service would be capable of rapidly rescheduling the ambulance and diverting it to respond to a different call.

Versatile Manufacturing

Manufacturing needs special attention. We shall have to substantially reduce outsourcing production and locate appropriately scaled manufacturing plants close to demand centres. This is now possible because we have AI technology for building cost-effective, smaller, *versatile* manufacturing plants—plants capable of producing a wide range of similar products.

The key requirement for the versatile manufacturing is to make all manufacturing resources—robots, machine tools and transporters—*reconfigurable*.

Whenever orders arrive for a product that is different from the one currently being produced, the versatile plant *self-organises* into an appropriate configuration, as follows:

Instantly detecting whether the requested product type is within the plant portfolio
Rapidly identifying which manufacturing resources are required
Configuring and scheduling the required resources

Knowhow how to build versatile manufacturing plants can be sold worldwide profitably and without harming the environment. Far better than selling and transporting the goods produced by these plants.

It is worth remembering though that before we can sell knowledge on how to manufacture, we must manufacture.

Gig Economy

The gig economy is a loosely connected network of individuals and groups who may work for several employers and enjoy the full freedom of deciding where, when, how long and with whom to work, giving up in the process the security and fringe benefits (such as paid holidays) offered by traditional full-time employment. The gig economy is like a set of virtual organisations; it spontaneously emerged as a reaction to the increased complexity of markets.

For those with rare skills, who are in high demand, participating in the gig economy is a valuable experience.

It is also a kind of a safety net—many unskilled workers made redundant during the prolonged pandemic crisis were glad for an opportunity to join the gig economy as the only way to find occasional part-time employment.

Who Is Who in the Emerging Digital Economy

The valuations of the new knowledge-based businesses, exemplified by Apple, Amazon, Google, Microsoft, Facebook and Tesla, are exceeding anything we saw in the past. In contrast, producers of industrial goods (General Motors, Ford) or energy (Shell, Exon, BP), once highly valued by the industrial society, are now pushed to the B list.

These valuations may be excessive and may be drastically reduced in a panic reaction of the market makers to an economic crisis, and yet, they will persist. It is a long-term trend.

Leaders in the Digital Transformation

Nations that complete the digital transformation of their businesses, healthcare and administrations without delay will prosper under the new complex economic conditions. The leading nation in digital transformation is the USA, which has a well-established digital business elite: Apple, Amazon, Google, Microsoft, Facebook, Intel, Instagram, Twitter, Zoom and Tesla.

In contrast, Europe has not a single high-value digital business.

The UK's digital strength is in a large number of small- to medium-sized digital businesses.

The most valuable digital businesses in the world by stock market valuation, at the time this text was written, July 2022, were:

USA
Apple—$2.4 trillion valuation generated by 150,000 employees
Microsoft—$2 trillion valuation generated by 180,000 employees
Google—$1.6 trillion valuation generated by 140,000 employees
Amazon—$1.1 trillion valuation generated by 1.3 million employees
Facebook—$840 billion valuation generated by 60,000 employees
Tesla—$800 billion valuation generated by 80,000 employees
China
Alibaba—$300 billion valuation; 118,000 employees
South Korea
Samsung—$300 billion valuation; 310,000 employees

What Has Happened to the Industrial Giants?

In comparison, manufacturers of cars (the elite of the industrial economy) are considerably less effective in terms of value generated per employee.

Consider the contrast:

Apple—$2.4 trillion valuation generated by 150,000 employees
Volkswagen—$130 billion valuation generated by 600,000 employees

Is It Important for a Nation to Create Disruptive Technologies?

Eminent economists have expressed the view that for a nation's economy, it is more important to have a large "footprint" of businesses using advanced technology than hosting the highly valued businesses that create disruptive technologies. The view, although it sounds plausible, neglects the historical fact—the nation of inventors always has the largest footprint of applications, at least initially. England at the beginning of the Industrial Revolution dominated the world economy, and the USA today, as the leader of digital revolution, has no meaningful economic competitor.

In addition, innovation leaders tend to retain creative power for a long time. Consider the reincarnation of Facebook as Meta, with the new radical goal to create the *metaverse*, the digital twin of the universe. The idea is to enable anyone equipped with special glasses to cross between the two worlds at will. Mark Zuckerberg's announcement that Meta will create in the near future 10,000 jobs may be an exaggeration; nevertheless, many new jobs will be created.

The advantage gained by inventing is, of course, not permanent. Early adopters may overtake the inventor.

Key Points

1. The legacy of industrial economy are very large corporations and administrations designed to operate in stable markets, which are not capable of coping with the sharply increased complexity of the Internet-based global market.
2. Legacy corporation and administrations could be transformed into adaptive, resilient and sustainable modern organisations (smart digital ecosystems) by the injection of a good dose of artificial intelligence (smart digital transformation).
3. Smart digital transformation, if undertaken in earnest, would create a substantial number of high-tech jobs and would result in transforming the UK economy into a high-tech, high-wage, high-productivity economy.
4. Another legacy of industrial economy is globalisation—building large-scale factories in faraway developing countries and transporting goods across continents to demand points—with unforeseen consequences of wasting energy and polluting the environment.
5. Smaller and versatile factory can be now built cost-effectively, manufacturing a wide range of similar products, and located close to demand points. AI-based schedulers can almost instantly reconfigure such a factory to switch production from one product to another within the specified range.
6. Countries with expertise in manufacturing advanced goods could export *knowledge* on how to manufacture goods, instead of exporting actual goods, drastically reducing consumption of energy as well as CO_2 production.

References

1. Schumacher, E. F. "Small is Beautiful: A Study of Economics as People Mattered". HarperCollins, 1973.
2. Rzevski, G., P. Skobelev, "Managing Complexity". WIT Press, Southampton, Boston, 2014. ISBN 978-1-84564-936-4.
3. Drucker, P., "The Age of Discontinuity". Butterworth-Heinemann, 1969.

7

The New Digital Society

Introduction

The key notion of complexity worldview is that the *future is not given*. It is not possible to precisely predict how digital technology will change the current society.

However, it is rather naïve to believe that the transition from the industrial to the digital society will be any less revolutionary than the preceding two major transitions—from the society of hunters and gatherers to agricultural society and from agricultural to industrial society.

I describe here my own vision of the emerging digital society in which knowledge rather than capital is the main resource for conducting business, participating in politics, offering education, providing healthcare and protecting the nation.

You can trust me on what digital technology will enable us to do, but don't necessarily accept my views on which opportunities will be taken forward and which ones will be ignored.

It is important to remember that *we have AI technology which could help us create a new society capable of providing food, water, housing, education, healthcare, employment and entertainment to all its members without harming the environment and, at the same time, offering individuals a considerable freedom to choose how to live, work and express themselves.*

© The Author(s), under exclusive license to Springer Nature Switzerland AG 2023
G. Rzevski, *The Future is Digital*, https://doi.org/10.1007/978-3-031-37810-2_7

Freedom to Choose

Digital technology enables individuals and groups to closely interact with others at a distance. This feature opens up exciting new possibilities—we don't have to follow strict routines of the industrial society such as 9 to 5 in the office or a factory, 5 days a week, all our working lives.

We shall be able to make choices. And if we make a mistake, wrong choices will be possible to change.

Choosing Your Own Lifestyle and Work Patterns

The most exciting new development is that participants in the knowledge economy can *choose the lifestyle* that suits them best—they can select where to live, because they can work from any location, including home, an office, a café or a hotel, or whilst travelling in trains, or planes, and they can adjust their working hours to fit into their general life pattern.

There is little doubt that *working from a distance (as a home worker or as a digital nomad) or in the offices near home will be a norm.* Businesses can save by closing expensive city centre offices, office workers will avoid long commuting, and reduced travel will have a positive impact on energy saving and the environment.

Employers will be able to hire knowledge workers who live in faraway countries and probably offer them office facilities near their homes.

It is likely that many will join virtual organisations, or the gig economy, but some will prefer less risky, well-protected working environment when working for a single employer.

The variety of lifestyles available to individuals will increase.

As online working, shopping, banking, socialising and entertainment increase in popularity, plans are being drawn to remodel town centres by converting office blocks, large department stores and even some small shops into flats and replace empty retail outlets with spaces for entertainment, sport, healthcare services, cafes, bars and restaurants, which will enable those of us who prefer to live in a city centre, rather than in the country, to do so.

Wherever one chooses to live, it is likely that there will be opportunities to live and work in small, connected communities. Schumacher was, almost, right—small is beautiful, but only *if connected.*

Creating Your Own Educational Programmes

Education at all levels, from primary to university, will change. Online learning, modelled on The Open University combined with the face-to-face tutorials, as offered by the Oxbridge colleges, will provide a high-value learning experience.

At universities and possibly even in the secondary education, students will be able, with the help from their tutors, to *design their own personal curricula* by selecting educational material from a vast library of high-quality online lectures, presentations, documentaries, electronic books and educational videos. In addition to working in the laboratories of their own university, students will be able to remotely access and conduct experiments online in laboratories belonging to other universities or research centres irrespective of their location and without a need to travel.

We are all different—each individual will have an opportunity to find their own right balance between online and face to face. The educational system must not be allowed to impose upon students one-for-all way of teaching.

Lifelong education, concurrent with work, will be a norm.

Creating Your Own Healthcare Programmes

It is quite clear that, monstrously large and managed by hierarchies of administrators, the UK National Health Service, which employs over 1.5 million people, will not survive the onslaught of complexity.

Once sanity prevails and the big, rigid structure is transformed into a network of smaller, patient-centred units, where the allocation of medical resources to medical demands is switched to AI-based real-time schedulers, and medical professionals are provided with AI-based analytics and diagnostic systems, we can expect that it would be feasible for doctors and patients to work out *personal healthcare programmes*, which will include preventive medicine.

Decline of Central Control

The excessive earning differences between chief executives and employees, which were a norm in industrial society (and still persist), are bound to be reduced in the new digital society in which we have to rely on the *intelligence of every knowledge worker* to deal with issues created by the complexity of our socioeconomic environment. In the new landscape, we are bound to experience distribution of responsibilities and, consequently, of remuneration, throughout businesses and administration. This trend will help to reduce inequality of income. It is difficult to imagine that knowledge workers would tolerate the current remuneration excesses.

Similarly in politics, leading a nation into digital society requires a variety of skills, which implies distribution of responsibilities and collective decision-making with a prime minister coordinating and helping to resolve conflicts rather than deciding how to allocate limited resources to many competing demands.

Declining importance of central control and the devolution of decision-making are key consequences of the recent sharp increase in complexity.

Switching to Issue-Based Political System and Direct Democracy?

In a fast-changing new world, it is hardly possible for rigid political parties, based on divisions valid in the industrial society—rich bosses versus poor wage earners—to survive much longer. After all, the knowledge-based service industry, when fully developed, will hardly require many manual industrial workers. Cleaning, plumbing, building repairs and catering service workers will be most probably organised around agents, like freelance artists.

At the time of writing this chapter—June 2022—this political evolution was already on the way. A considerable number of working-class voters in the UK supported the Conservative Party, and a similar-size section of middle-class voters voted for the Labour Party. But a really dramatic change occurred in France, where two traditionally strongest parties, Socialists of the Left and Republicans of the Right, collapsed.

Left-right-based political system—socialists versus capitalists—will not make sense in the complex digital society with major national issues continuously changing. And capitalism is anyway soon to be replaced with post-capitalist knowledge economy.

Nobody can currently say with certainty what shape the new political system will have. My guess is that it will be *issue-oriented* and will evolve as issues change.

In the UK, we have recently experienced several serious issue-based national divisions, which went across left-right party lines.

For and against Brexit
For and against government-imposed strict movement restrictions during Covid
For and against steep net-zero targets
Free speech versus cancel culture

As we switch to issue-based political system, it is likely that major national issues will be settled by direct voting like in Switzerland, the model country in which the German, French and Italian population live in harmony with each other and with recent immigrants, which is organised in cantons (in other words—*clusters*) and is offering opportunities to every citizen to vote directly on how major national issues should be resolved.

Changing the Social and Political Elite

Throughout the social evolution, those in charge of the key economic resource were privileged—landowners in agricultural society and wealthy in industrial society. There is little doubt that in the new knowledge-based services, society knowledge will bring privileges.

As the knowledge economy develops, knowledge workers will gradually broaden their interests and socio-political awareness and will aspire to participate more actively in the democratic processes.

New personalities in the news are Bill Gates, Tim Cook, Jeff Bezos, Mark Zuckerberg and Elon Musk. They acquired their eminence and unprecedented wealth in a very short time by creating early digital businesses through invention, clearly demonstrating the notion that *knowledge is today more important as an economic resource than money.* They and their successors will be the new social and political elite.

It is not possible to lead a nation into the digital future with an industrial era mindset.

The current establishment will, of course, resist the takeover, and the struggle may last many years, but, in the end, the digital society will prevail, and leaders of digital transformation will become the establishment.

History of drastic social changes experienced when the agricultural society was replaced by the industrial, when aristocrats and landowners had to hand over political power to capitalists, will be repeated.

Digitising Care for the Ageing Population

Our ageing population, contrary to general belief, is not a burden for the young—it is an opportunity for them to design and produce a variety of *AI-enabled care systems*, from self-driving trolleys to intelligent housekeeping, heating, cooling, ventilation, lighting, healthcare, communication and security systems. Japan already has a comprehensive strategy for converting the savings of their retired population into investments for the development of digital caring technology, which they call Society 5.0 [1].

In the UK, a digital healthcare start-up, CERA, uses advanced digital technology to provide healthcare services at home reducing hospitalisation by 52%.

AI and Military

I believe that wars are unnecessary and cruel. Conflicts must be possible to resolve by negotiation and patience. Nevertheless, in a complex world, it is prudent to maintain *high-quality defence force*.

Let's consider what complexity science and AI can do for improving defence performance and, at the same time, reducing its costs.

As a start, we have to realise that, in the twenty-first century, *warfare is a complex system* and, in accordance with the law of requisite complexity, the defence must be designed to have the appropriate complexity (Chap. 2). The implication is that it should be centrally *coordinated* rather than controlled and should consist of diverse and partially autonomous *defence missions* engaged in intensive interaction.

The allocation of defence resources, human, physical and financial, to defence missions, could be cost-effectively done by digital twins of defence missions, as described in Chap. 4.

Emergent AI could greatly improve defence adaptiveness and resilience by rapidly and consistently making low-risk decisions, particularly in logistic, purchasing of defence resources and mission deployment.

And, of course, AI could enable the construction of self-driving, self-piloting and self-navigating weapons.

Defence against cyberattacks is another area ready to expand where AI will have a crucial role.

Key Points

1. Digital society will provide individuals with an increased freedom to choose how to work and live and encourage them to create their own educational and healthcare programmes.
2. Central control will be in decline in politics and in business and will be replaced by the devolution of decision-making to as many partially autonomous clusters of participants, or individuals, as practical.
3. We shall live, most probably, in direct democracies based on referendums and the evolving, issue-based, political action groups.
4. In time, knowledge workers will take over the establishment.

Reference

1. Fukuda, K, "Science, technology and innovation ecosystem transformation toward society 5.0". International Journal of Production Economics, Elsevier, vol. 220, 2020. 107460.

Key Points

Let's accentuate the main points of the book—ideas that readers are expected to absorb and apply.

1. **Coevolution of society and technology proceeds in distinct steps, and *the next step is digital.***

   The humanity has experienced three distinct societies—society of hunters and gatherers, agricultural society and industrial society—and is now *in transition to digital society* (also known as information society).

   The sharp increase of complexity of the world in transition masks the pattern of social evolution. Voters, badly affected by consequences of extreme events such as the Covid pandemic and the invasion of Ukraine, blame politicians, who are really not in control.

   Readers of this book should be able to recognise the correct evolutionary pattern—the transition from industrial to digital society—although it is hidden in the mass of data and false interpretations.

2. **Coevolution of society and technology is unstoppable and irreversible, but *it can be tweaked*.**

   Whilst we can recognise broad patterns of evolution, it is not possible to predict what exactly will happen in each individual country.

© The Author(s), under exclusive license to Springer Nature Switzerland AG 2023
G. Rzevski, *The Future is Digital*, https://doi.org/10.1007/978-3-031-37810-2

It is up to each nation to decide whether to encourage and stimulate digital progress or to delay it from the fear of the unknown aftereffects, which may be brought about by powerful digital tools, such as artificial intelligence.

Countries that decide to race into the digital future will need to devise digital strategy based on the following three elements.

Creating economic growth by focusing on digital services and AI
Gradually withdrawing from globalisation and maximising national self-sufficiency
Ensuring that the prosperity created by digital industry is shared among all

3. **Complexity of our political, social and economic environments is not going away—it is actually increasing. Without embracing the complexity worldview, it will be difficult to live and prosper in a complex world**.

Complexity does create negative issues, but, most importantly, it offers new opportunities to those who thrive under conditions of uncertainty. The imperative is to accept that stable and predictable world is not going to return soon, if ever, and to re-tune our worldview to embrace complexity.

4. **AI is neither friend nor foe—*AI is just a very smart tool*; people who use AI for unethical purposes are foes.**

It wouldn't be wise to stop or delay developing and using AI.

Artificial intelligence is an excellent tool for managing complexity and has immense potential for helping us to create a high-value, high-productivity, high-wage economy as well as the cost-effective healthcare and educational services. Let's make supporting AI the top priority.

The perceived danger of AI taking over the world is currently remote. If you have any doubt, please reread the part of Chap. 3 in which the might of the human brain is compared to current modest artificial neural networks.

Let's better focus on devising effective legislation for penalising people who train and use AI for unethical activities.

5. **In a complex world, *adaptability and resilience* are critical success factors**.

When the socioeconomic environment is volatile and unpredictable, and there is an increased risk of fraud and cyberattacks, it is essential to be able to instantly identify the occurrence of any disruptive event, to rapidly assess its impact and to reschedule available resources to prevent, or at least minimise, losses. In other words, to be adaptive and resilient.

The advice is equally appropriate for national and local governments, state-owned and private enterprises and even for individuals—continuously observe your environment and keep re-evaluating both aspirations and actions.

6. **To prosper in a complex environment, traditional organisations should be transformed into *digital ecosystems*.**

Large and rigid corporations and administrations designed to operate in stable environments cannot rapidly respond to frequent unpredictable disruptive events. Their long lines of command and reporting are just too slow, and decision-makers are far from where the action is.

By employing AI to replace human operational decision-makers, the response time to disruptions can be drastically reduced and the speed of potential damage assessment and rescheduling of resources significantly increased, making the enterprise adaptive and resilient—genuine digital ecosystem.

7. **Trading in knowledge rather than in goods reduces pollution, saves energy and ensures national self-sufficiency in critical goods.**

Locating very large factories in remote countries far from demand points, to take advantage of cheap labour, creates exceedingly long global supply chains and generates excessive business travel which, in turn, wastes energy, escalates pollution and, most importantly, increases vulnerability of nations in times of global crises, such as pandemics or wars.

To shorten supply chains, we should build AI-driven, versatile, small-scale manufacturing plants and locate them near the points of consumption.

The trading in knowledge-based services will largely, but not completely, replace trading in goods. The trend is already evident—according to Statista, in 2021, services formed 77.6% of the GDP of the USA, the undisputable digital leader.

Printed in the United States
by Baker & Taylor Publisher Services